Reasonably Happy

Copyright © Paul Ollinger 2024
All rights reserved.

This book is packed with essays meant to make you go *haha* or *ah ha!*, not to be taken as financial or psychological advice. The author is a comedian, not a financial advisor or therapist—so while the jokes might crack you up, they're not going to help you balance your portfolio or work through your childhood issues. If you're making major life decisions or trying to understand the depths of your mind, please consult a professional. Don't swap your therapist for this book, unless your therapist is into comedy too, then make them buy their own.

ISBN 978-0-9972706-5-5 (paperback)
ISBN 978-0-9972706-6-2 (ebook)

Publisher's Cataloging-in-Publication Data

Names: Ollinger, Paul, author.
Title: Reasonably happy : money , work , and life / Paul Ollinger.
Description: New York, NY: Absolutely Huge Books, 2024.
Identifiers: LCCN: 2024916657 | ISBN: 978-0-9972706-5-5 (paperback) | 978-0-9972706-6-2 (ebook)
Subjects: LCSH Success. | Success in business. | Self actualization (Psychology)--Humor. | Conduct of life--Humor. | Essays. | BISAC HUMOR / Topic / Business & Professional | BUSINESS & ECONOMICS / Personal Success | SELF-HELP / Personal Growth / Happiness | LITERARY COLLECTIONS / Essays
Classification: LCC PN6231.P785 O55 2024 | DDC 818/.607--dc23
Book design by Adam Robinson

First published by Absolutely Huge Books in 2024
www.paulollinger.com

Essays on Money, Work, and Other Things that Piss Me Off

PAUL OLLINGER

Absolutely Huge Books
New York, New York

Contents

Introduction   xiii

MONEY

Money, Pain, and New Cars	3
How to Be Rich, According to the Happiest Country in the World	7
The Real Reason It's Called "F-You Money"	11
The Secret to Being Very, Very Rich	15
Nobody Needs a House with 8 Toilets	19
Money Isn't What You're Missing	23
The Streaming Services Cluster*ck	27
31 Flavors of Comcast (a one-act play)	33
Adventures in Affluence: Dry Cleaning	37
We Are All Phil Mickelson	41

WORK

Dare to Suck	47
The Pandemic Proved That Work Is a Privilege	51
Gary v. Jerry	55
Why Comedy Clubs Matter	59
How to Host a Traveling Comedian	63
Dear Podcast Publicist…	67
The Thing Malcolm Gladwell Forgot to Mention	71
The Best Worst Interview Advice Ever	75
The Dreaded H-Word	79
Managing Sales Quota Stress	83
Mid-Career Burnout Is Real	87
White Whale Career Metaphor Acid Dream	91
Guardrails Are Good	95
Burn Your Boats!	99
An Inadequate Tribute to Dave Goldberg	105

LIFE

Every Day Is Thanksgiving	111
This Is Us	115
Why the Jews?	119
What My Dad's Death Taught Me About Life	125
Lessons from a Freshman Pimple	129
Why Talking About Money and Happiness Matters	133
A Stoic Thought Exercise: What if it All Goes Away?	137
Life Is Short. Take a Swing.	141
Nightmare on the Back Nine	145
The Sunk Cost of Thanksgiving Leftovers	149
Staying Hungry When Your Life is Full	153
Stop Keeping Score	157
Don't Take a Break from Social Media. Manage It.	159
You Deserve It!	163
Why Marriage is Hard	167
The Future is Analog: Learn to Fight	171
Your Neighbors Are Your World	175
Toilet Paper as Societal Barometer	179
Want to Be Happier? Check the Thesaurus	183
Don't Live Every Day as if it's Your Last	187
Your Only Goal Is to Arrive	191
Acknowledgements	195

For Stacey

ADVANCE PRAISE FOR REASONABLY HAPPY

"Paul Ollinger's new book, *Reasonably Happy*, is a fabulous blend of wit and wisdom. Paul is a genuinely funny writer yet what really recommends this book is one profound insight after another into our humanity—how we love, work, spend, and sometimes just goof around. In a delightfully irreverent tone that never takes itself too seriously, each bite-sized chapter is a chance to reflect, grow, and—yes—laugh."

— **BRIAN PORTNOY**, CFA, PhD, author *The Geometry of Wealth*

"Paul's brainy, relatable comedy had me in stitches when I saw him on stage. In *Reasonably Happy*, he had me laughing out loud by the 4th sentence. His observations on money, work, and life are irreverent and truly delightful."

— **DR. BRAD KLONTZ**, Author and TikTok Superstar @DrBradKlontz

"In *Reasonably Happy*, Paul Ollinger has done the exceptional, wrapping financial wisdom with humor, insight and rich storytelling. It serves as a fresh reminder that true wealth comes from balancing both your wallet and your well-being…and holding space for laughter."

— **FARNOOSH TORABI**, host of *So Money* and author of *A Healthy State of Panic*

"A sparkling collection of writings about money, work, and life—and this is coming from someone who writes a lot about money, work, and life. Mostly lighthearted—but deadly serious at times—these snappy essays are a subtle but firm nudge for you to start making positive changes in your life. There is nothing in here that is fake or inauthentic, and you'll find yourself belly-laughing or nodding in agreement."

— **JARED DILLIAN**, author of *No Worries: How To Live a Stress-Free Financial Life*

"In *Reasonably Happy*, Paul Ollinger plays the role of Shakespeare's court jester, using humor to deliver hard-hitting truths about money, work, and life. While you're laughing through stories about dental work, how bad Comcast sucks, and the miracle of Thanksgiving (among others), you'll find yourself confronting life's deeper realities. Paul wields essays like the jester wields jokes; he's slyly teaching you valuable lessons without you even realizing it."

— **JOE SAUL-SEHY**, Host, Stacking Benjamins podcast

"Paul Ollinger would be a terrible drug dealer—he's far too honest about the diminishing returns. It's the kind of financial advice that won't make you rich but might make you happier. Paul delivers financial wisdom with a comedian's wit, making you laugh while rethinking your life choices."

— **TURNEY DUFF**, *New York Times* bestselling author of *The Buy Side*

Introduction

This project started because I wanted to create a tangible souvenir for audience members to take away from my live comedy shows. My hope was to establish a connection with potential fans, and to help answer the most common question people ask at brunch the morning following my comedy shows: "Honey, the comedian we saw last night, what was his name?"

20 years ago, most comics' merch consisted of DVDs or audio CDs, which were easy to transport and—unlike t-shirts—came in only one size. Now they're obsolete. So I'm aware of the irony of re-purposing this online content in printed form. But I like the idea that, similar to a recording of a live show, a collection of essays is a sample of how the performer thinks about the world. That doesn't mean the millions of people who buy this book will actually read it, but it's nice to think that they *might*.

Before I dug into my file of old articles, I wondered if I'd have sufficient material to get this book past an anemic page count. But as I scoured the work that I've published over the past decade on *HuffPo*, *Entrepreneur*, LinkedIn, *The Commercial Appeal*, *Medium*, *FORGE*, and Substack, I was surprised at how much I found. Sure, I'm not cranking out a weekly column for the *New York Times*, but the scope and quality demonstrated that, if you keep at something over time, it adds up.

Some themes arose. There was a lot of material about Covid and quarantine. Maybe I found more time to write when the comedy clubs were closed, or maybe this unfortunate period catalyzed my reflection. Whatever it was, reviewing those pieces reminds me to be grateful that it's (mostly) behind us. My only hope here is that, should the universe present us with another, similar disaster, we get to go through it in our pajamas again.

These pandemic articles demonstrated a challenge about any retrospective collection: items written in the present tense will read differently at some point in the future. References to my age or the age of my children are relevant but fleeting. Whether writing about Thanksgiving leftovers, a societal shutdown, or the death of my father, context and temporal proximity matters. In a few cases, we changed the tense to make reading as easy and logical as possible.

So, it was nice meeting you last night. If you thought I was funny, here's a peek into my brain that you can take with you on a plane, or leave on the back of your toilet. And tell all your friends my name is Paul Ollinger (ahh'-lin-jurr).

MONEY

Money, Pain, and New Cars

The diminishing analgesic effects of wealth
SUBSTACK, APRIL 2023

When I was 12 years old, my dad took me to the dentist to get my first cavity filled. "By the way," he said as we walked into the office, "don't get the Novocaine—it's $20."

My father was a very good man—the most decent, humble person I've ever known. But he was so frugal and required so little material fulfillment in his own life that maybe he had trouble understanding other people's desire for teeny-tiny luxuries like anesthesia.

Ten minutes later, as Dr. Stalling's drill tore into my virgin molar and the acrid stench of pulverized tooth filled the air, I writhed in agony and dug my fingernails into the arm of the dental chair. Then and there, I made myself a promise: "Someday, I'm going to make some damn money." Because, in certain cases, money literally relieves pain.

I was thinking about this the other day while driving my new car. After ten years, I traded in my Tesla for a Mercedes SUV. It's a beautiful piece of German engineering (by way of Alabama), and I still get excited when I see it. However, as tasty as my new ride is, it's nowhere close to the most thrilling automobile purchase I have ever made. That honor belongs to the 1994 Saturn SL2.

In 1994, I was three years out of college, and the real world was kicking my butt. My employer paid me a whopping $25,000 salary, but, thanks to repair bills on the 12-year-old Honda Accord I drove,

I had already incurred $4,000 in credit card debt. This would be over $8,000 in 2024 dollars, a seemingly insurmountable balance.

Hondas are famous for being reliable, but mine was possessed by the devil. Every morning when I turned the key, it was a game of will she or won't she start? While I idled at stop lights, I heard the nausea-inducing pings, clunks, and crunches that foreshadowed another $800 invoice from Vinny the Mechanic. Dread was my co-pilot.

A car is often an outward sign of how its owner's life is going. With a cracked windshield, a temperamental transmission, and an A/C that blew only dirt and dead spiders, my vehicle's accurate signals did not enhance my dating life, especially in the sticky heat of Memphis, TN. No young woman riding shotgun and sweating through her Counting Crows t-shirt ever thinks, "I gotta make babies with this winner!"

But good news lurked on the horizon! By hitting a few ambitious goals at work, I earned myself a promotion and a $7,500 raise (30% bump, baby!), which allowed me to finance an automobile.

Thus did I acquire a shiny, new Saturn SL2 on a Sunday afternoon from a salesman with a John Stossel mustache. The transaction drastically improved my life, delivering transportational serenity in a way none of my subsequent luxury car purchases would, regardless of the massive disparity in amenities.

Consider this: my SUV is loaded with a 362-HP engine, leather interior, 20" spoke wheels, a symphony-quality sound system, and seats that blow chilled air up my crack. My Saturn, on the other hand, was a tin can with bicycle tires, a moped engine, and AM/FM cassette player. Yet, as unsexy as Salty the Saturn was, I loved her.

Why? Easy—she started when asked, ran without complaint, and sipped gas with teetotalling restraint. But most of all, Salty removed chaos from my life. Instead of the pain of repair bills, I had a predictable and very reasonable monthly car payment. Instead of jungle-caliber humidity, I had air conditioning. Instead of a cringe-inducing junker, I had a shot with the ladies.

Before you say, "money won't make you happy," qualify it with the phrase "beyond a certain point." A recent Bankrate survey found that

56% of Americans can't cover a $1,000 emergency expense with their savings. That means more than half of us are constantly navigating an endless series of financial crises. When their car breaks down, they get a speeding ticket, or have a fender-bender, they are screwed. If you told these folks that money—say $5,000—wouldn't improve their life, they would laugh in your clueless face. It might not solve all their problems, but it would get them through the month.

When you live on the cusp of financial chaos, every step away from the economic abyss relieves pain: the fear of uncertainty, the lack of self-determination, and the doubt in oneself. Of course, this pain is psychic as opposed to physical, but it is every bit as real as having one's bicuspid decimated by a spinning metal spike.

At lower economic levels, small increments of money deliver narcotic bliss and push us away from threats to our subsistence. But as we save money and build wealth, additional funds contribute less and less to our overall well-being. Economists call this decreasing marginal utility, and—to me—there's no better example than buying new cars.

Going from a beater like my old Honda to a reliable new Saturn is a booster rocket for your self-esteem. But when you trade in a used Tesla for a new Mercedes, you are not extinguishing pain. You're just drizzling a little extra chocolate sauce on the ice cream sundae that is your life. The danger here is that—because it doesn't provide the same exhilaration as past purchases—we forget how amazing it is to *not* have imminent catastrophe riding in the backseat.

You can't appreciate this lack of chaos in your life if you don't notice it. So the next time your car starts, think, "this is good." When you drive past the mechanic who used to have you over a barrel, say out loud, "not anymore, Vinny." And if you ever feel a comfy breeze blowing up your skirt or trousers, remind yourself just how far up Maslow's Hierarchy of Automotive Needs you're living.

There's nothing better than self-determination, which is what my Saturn represented to me. I was solving real-world problems and figuring out life as an adult. It was Novocaine for my soul, and I'll never forget it.

How to Be Rich, According to the Happiest Country in the World

Meik Wiking, author of The Little Book of Hygge, *tells us what the Danes know about converting wealth into well-being*

MEDIUM, OCTOBER 2020

Winters in Copenhagen are long and dreary. Denmark's tax rates are legitimately scary. And Hamlet was a bit glum, to say the least. But year after year, the Danes place at or near the top of the World Happiness Report, a global ranking that uses Gallup World Poll data to measure contentment by country.

In comparison with Denmark, the United States seems like it should score much better on a happiness test. Winters here are, on average, far more temperate. Our tax rates are relatively benign. And boy, do we have a lot of resources to entertain ourselves, from 23 Six Flags amusement parks to a near-monopoly on Cheesecake Factory restaurants. Despite this, we keep coming in around 18th or 19th on the list. This year, we're sandwiched between Germany and the Czech Republic.

I wanted to find out what the Danes know that the rest of us don't, and, more selfishly, how I could implement some Danish happiness practices in my life. So I invited Meik Wiking, the CEO and founder of Denmark's Happiness Research Institute and the author of the international bestseller, *The Little Book of Hygge: Danish Secrets to Happy Living,* to join me in conversation on my podcast. If you've heard of *hygge* (pronounced roughly "hoo'i-guh"), it very well may have been in relation to this book.

Wiking and I discussed how the difference between Danish and American happiness is a function of what we value. Speaking generally, Danes emphasize togetherness, their social safety net, and work-life balance. "Nordic countries are really good at converting their wealth into well-being," he told me. "They invest in things and experiences that create good conditions for good lives."

In contrast, Americans glorify individualism, affluence, and achievement. It's why millions of us spend 70 hours a week at jobs that feel inauthentic to who we are and what we want. This attitude doesn't seem to be changing with the next generation. In one recent peer-reviewed study, three-quarters of first-year college students ranked "being very well off financially" as essential or important, a percentage that exceeds that of Gen X and is 68% higher than that of baby boomers. Of all the goals the survey asked the students to assess, including developing a meaningful philosophy of life, keeping up with politics, and creating art, being rich remained the top priority.

The more Wiking and I discussed our respective countries' approach to life, the more I thought about the mega-author, talk show host, and marriage whisperer Dr. Phil. (I promise it'll make sense in a minute.)

If you've ever watched Dr. Phil's talk show, you'll recognize a trick he uses to get his guests to see the errors in their marital argument tactics. The guest—usually the husband—can't resolve his domestic disagreements because he insists his point of view is logically correct. At which point, Dr. Phil breaks out his signature Socratic question. Kindly, but firmly, he asks, "Do you want to be right…or do you want to be happy?"

In those few words, he elegantly contrasts an apparently self-evident positive (being right) against a far more important objective (being happy). Here's why this is relevant to the question of Danish happiness: the idea that riches and professional status are self-evident positives is ingrained deeply into American culture. It's a belief I held firmly for most of my life. Yet we spend very little time considering whether affluence or status actually leads to life satisfaction.

Let's channel Dr. Phil to see if we can achieve Danish-style well-being. Instead of wondering, "How do I get promoted?" or "How do I make more money?" a better question might be: "What do I need to be happy?"

When we start to put serious time into finding an answer, it becomes clear that, to some degree, happiness is a choice. Barring illness and tragedy, we have a much better chance of being happy when we cultivate an awareness of the true sources of satisfaction and choose to prioritize them over sparkling objects that don't deliver.

This is where the Danes do so well. Danish culture values both authentic work and work-life balance, two factors that have a big impact on our happiness. "A lot of miserable millionaires spend their lives working on something they don't enjoy just because they can make a bit more money," Wiking says. The Danish way: "Listen to your gut and to where your passion is."

Of course, you might not be able to change careers in an afternoon, but there are small ways we can generate happiness every single day. For example, Danes emphasize spending time with loved ones—more than any other EU country, as Wiking points out in his book. That might sound inconsequential, or like Danish propaganda, but it is neither. According to the Harvard Study of Adult Development, an eight-decade longitudinal study analyzing the circumstances that lead to wellness, social relationships are a massive indicator of health, happiness, and life expectancy. (Thus, the decision to visit with friends instead of plopping on the couch and watching Netflix not only makes you happier but can also help you live longer.)

So, when the Danes get together, they do it right, running the hygge playbook, which Wiking explains as "the art of creating a nice atmosphere." They light candles and a fire, turn on music, and lay out a buffet that is not only delicious but conducive to conversation. They create moments where they can savor togetherness, relaxation, and some simple pleasures, which add up to a truly rich lifestyle. Just thinking about it makes me want to put on a big sweater and some Dave Brubeck.

When things aren't going so well, Wiking adds, the same Danish values also provide a three-step prescription to turn the day around: "In Denmark, we have sort of a mental health [checklist]: Do something active. Do something together with other people. Do something meaningful."

In other words, your actions toward feeling better do not have to be heroic or pricey. Improving one's mood can be as simple as asking a friend to go for a walk or registering for a volunteer activity, anything to get you outside and out of your head.

Despite their high happiness scores, it seems the Danes don't have any proprietary secrets after all. They are just more intentional than other countries about creating experiences and crafting positive environments. You and I can increase our own well-being by replicating some of these simple behaviors. After learning about hygge, I have started lighting candles in my home office every morning and building dinnertime fires twice as often. Maybe this generates happiness because the family gathers to chat beside the toasty hearth. Or maybe there's something primal and satisfying in our relationship to flame. But I promise you this: fire delivers.

So does reaching out. During the pandemic, my wife and I became proactive about hosting safe social engagements on our back porch where, despite the social distance, we could share wine, laughter, and good conversation with our neighbors. It was a simple pleasure—certainly no trip to Six Flags with Dr. Phil, but it made us happy. And that should be the goal.

The Real Reason It's Called "F-You Money"

One of many secrets rich people won't tell you
SUBSTACK, JANUARY 2023

"The success comes, and you're on your own. There's no manual. One day, they give you a check…that you can't even relate to the zeros on the end, and you can get in a lot of trouble with that much money."

—*Tom Petty*

I went to business school because I wanted to make a lot of money. There were other legitimate reasons, but that was the driving factor.

One day during my first year, a classmate shared the news that the company where his dad worked had just gone public and now his dad had "fuck you money" (FU$). He elaborated: "Meaning, he now has sufficient cash to tell his boss 'F-you!' and live with the consequences."

"Wow," I said, blown away by the concept. "That's amazing!"

At the time, I was carrying today's equivalent of $150,000 in student debt, so any degree of financial independence sounded pretty cool. But to be so rich as not to need a job? That was incomprehensible.

Broke as I was, I didn't know what I didn't know about money. However, as too many lottery winners, young pro athletes, and yours truly learned after my own financial windfall, FU$ comes with more complications than you might think. While it grants the recipient a massive degree of freedom in both career and lifestyle, it also comes with rights, duties, and responsibilities, which—if not fully understood—can lead its owner down the wrong path. Very few other people will be so foolishly candid as to tell you this.

Consider your friendly, neighborhood Spider-Man: Peter Parker gets bit by a radioactive spider, thus endowing him with supernatural arachnoid capabilities. Isn't he lucky? Because now he does whatever a spider can, climbs skyscrapers, and catches thieves just like flies. He's in a whole new league.

But those extraordinary capabilities also distort his relationship with his career, his co-workers, his day-to-day life. Once a person can swing from buildings and capture crooks with sticky wrist jizz, how will he tolerate flying coach to Milwaukee for the 30th Annual Packaging Materials Supply Chain Management Convention? (Yes, we are re-casting Peter as a mid-level logistics manager.)

He can't. And tolerance—especially late in a career—is an essential workplace skill. Maybe Peter won't make a big deal of it right away, but eventually, he's going to let his lame, non-superhero supervisor know that he's effing Spider-Man. And Spider-Man doesn't go to cardboard conferences! Here's where Peter's quarterly performance reviews get awkward.

This is what it's like to win, earn, or otherwise acquire FU$. Having the ability *not* to work distorts one's relationship *with* work. Pumped up by the superpower of wealth, a person's ego starts to talk smack about work's indignities and their sneaky, duplicitous boss. Left unchecked, new money will start making decisions on its owner's behalf, and these decisions are rarely prudent.

Of course, FU$ is a tremendous privilege, but it is also a Career Detonator you won't even know you're carrying. Unless you purposefully embrace the ways work enriches your life—for example, by providing a place to contribute to the world among your gifted colleagues—your professional future teeters one spark of indiscretion away from a meth lab-caliber explosion. Because, without you even knowing it, FU$ has switched your mouth's safety lock to the "off" position, making it much harder to keep shut—especially if you were pre-disposed to run it in the first place.

When your boss outlines the itinerary for the Milwaukee paper conference, which she regrets she will be unable to attend, you'll find yourself thinking, "Wait a minute, I'm rich. This bullshit is optional." In such a scenario, you better learn that "FU$" doesn't just *grant you the right* to say "F.U." to your boss. It also means that if you haven't thought clearly about what your values are and who you want to be, if you haven't thought about the responsibilities that come with new wealth, you *will* tell your boss—and maybe your spouse and other family members as well—to F right off.

Of course, you could take the high road. You could decline her invitation, firmly but respectfully, and plan a graceful job departure that preserves future professional optionality. But where's the fun in nuance when you can go nuclear?

So, you light up the boss in a conflagration of candor. Spittle-flying, you call out her shortcomings with gerund-laced eloquence, documenting her hypocrisy and tyranny so thoroughly that you believe your co-workers will rally around you and place a crown on your head. Instead, they pull a Bay of Pigs and run for cover.

Your opponent appears unfazed as she wipes the verbal guano from her chin, admires her filthy fingers, and replies with serpentine satisfaction, "Thanks for being transparent." Then it dawns on you: this is the final entry on your LinkedIn profile.

As Dr. Phil would say, "How's it feel to be right?"

In a time of acute inequality, it is beyond taboo to talk openly about affluence. So instead of discussing the connection between our values and who we want to be when the money arrives, we leave it to the Kardashians to model wealth for us. No wonder so many newly rich people quit their jobs, bail on their marriages, and buy a bunch of superfluous crap.

In service of these fortunate, hard-working, good-saving people, some of whom will eventually achieve 100% career flexibility, I offer the most important lesson about FU$:

Just because you *can* tell your boss to fuck off, that doesn't mean you should.

The Secret to Being Very, Very Rich

Few people have what it takes
SUBSTACK, JUNE 2023

"Don't confuse desire with compulsion."

—*Felix Dennis*

If you want to be rich, you have to be unreasonable. You have to do things outside the realm of practicality, safety, and politeness. Because, to earn vast wealth, you must be compulsively driven toward that singular goal. Nothing else matters.

So claimed Felix Dennis, the late founder of *Maxim* magazine and Dennis Publishing, in his book *How to Get Rich*. Dennis doesn't come at the subject with the run-of-the-mill guidance of other "get rich" authors, almost none of whom enjoys a net worth anywhere near the £400mm Dennis had earned when he published his guide in 2008 (when the GBP was double its current value).

Perhaps that's why Dennis' advice feels so savagely authentic. Instead of preaching about dollar-cost-averaging or portfolio diversification, Dennis offers the reader unvarnished insights into building and preserving ownership of a company—aka, the only way to go from zero to very rich without being able to monetize your talents like Tom Brady, Taylor Swift, or J.K. Rowling.

As Dennis demonstrates through dozens of anecdotes and insights, maintaining control of any entity worth controlling will drive you past the brink of reasonability time and again. Thus does he come to one of his main rules for success: *don't confuse desire with compulsion*. Sure, everybody wants to have a lot of money (the desire), but very few people are willing or able to do whatever it takes to fulfill that vision (the compulsion).

Being unreasonably compulsive starts with resisting the siren song of a salaried career. Working for someone else—even in the C-suite—might make you very comfortable, but it won't make you very rich, which he defines as starting at $100 million in liquid assets. Forsaking life as an employee might sound romantic, but try turning down a predictable income when you're living in squalor and your very patient girlfriend is threatening to walk.

Even if you're down for this precarious path, you still need an idea that has the potential to grow into a thriving business, and the moxie to get the ball rolling. Then you have to go out into the world with the thickest of skins and walk the "narrow, lonely road to get the capital to make it so," a journey that Dennis found plagued with desperation and vultures.

But our hero's journey has only just begun. Beyond this, Dennis says, a founder must refuse to give in. You can't crumble when creditors have you by the bollocks. You must not fold when key employees conspire to wrest away a piece of your enterprise. You have to scrap, improvise, and cajole to make payroll when cash flows trickle. You've got to resist the tempting lucre when private equity guys make a juicy offer for 51% of your venture. In short, you positively, absolutely must maintain control, no matter what.

All of this will take a profound toll on your personal life because, if you want to achieve mega-wealth, work must trump relationships every single time. "Any distraction whatever can cost you a chance that may not come again," Dennis explains. "And, for the purposes of this book, family, lovers, and friends are distractions. Plain and simple."

It made me wonder whether being a billionaire also requires you to be an asshole. I don't think so, but it seems clear that you need to be willing to have others call you an asshole. Being unreasonably committed to achieving your goals means foregoing a conventional lifestyle and saying no when "good manners" would suggest saying yes.

This will provide ample evidence to those with relatively mediocre financial results that your gains are ill-gotten. 99.8% of people—me very much included—can't wrap their minds around the monomaniacal focus required to succeed at this scale. And because it's harder to accept this reality than to contrive an explanation for the yawning gap between your results and theirs, expect others to disparage your character, question your commitment to your children, suggest you broke the law or took advantage of others to rise to such heights.

Yes, if you want to be very rich, you'll need to be okay with people talking shit about you behind your back, to your face, on social media, and in the press. Because once it's clear you will become crazy wealthy, you also become, in other people's eyes, an inhuman circus freak onto whom they project their insecurities and the bourgeois values to which they are suddenly so committed. There's no better example of this than the politicians and activists who chant, "Billionaires should not exist!"

Pondering Dennis' words helps me put my own situation into perspective. Had I stayed in the technology industry for another five years, I probably would have made it to the nine-figure club. But my commitment to hitting that number wasn't sufficiently unreasonable. I wasn't having fun; I didn't want to work so hard; I wanted to help care for my aging parents and to give comedy a full swing. These are all very understandable, very *reasonable* goals that perfectly demonstrate the difference between desire and compulsion.

When I find myself coveting the trappings of the super-rich or thinking snarky thoughts about Messrs. Musk or Bezos, I try to remember that their stratospheric success in no way diminishes my choices and accomplishments. They picked an unreasonable path and reaped unreasonable rewards. Good for them. Felix Dennis would be proud.

Nobody Needs a House with 8 Toilets

The declining marginal returns of real estate
SUBSTACK, JUNE 2023

I grew up in a house with eight people and three toilets. You're smart, so you've probably already done the math in your head:

8 people/3 Toilets = .375 Toilets Per Person (TPP)

Considered from a global perspective, this represents a plethora of porcelain! But international wealth equality is not on the mind of a ten-year-old who is trying not to pee his pants while one of his three sisters is locked in the bathroom curling her hair.

This scarcity-induced trauma instilled in me a lifelong yearning for lavatorial autonomy. So it should come as no surprise that today I live in a house with eight toilets to serve its four residents. Now my wife, kids, and I are literally surrounded by toilets (see image).

While I am happier to have more choices, five times as many toilets per person has not rewarded me with 500% more life satisfaction. It's definitely better, but it's also a comical reminder that we often overspend on crap—sometimes literally—with the idea that buying the things we lack will get us closer to personal fulfillment.

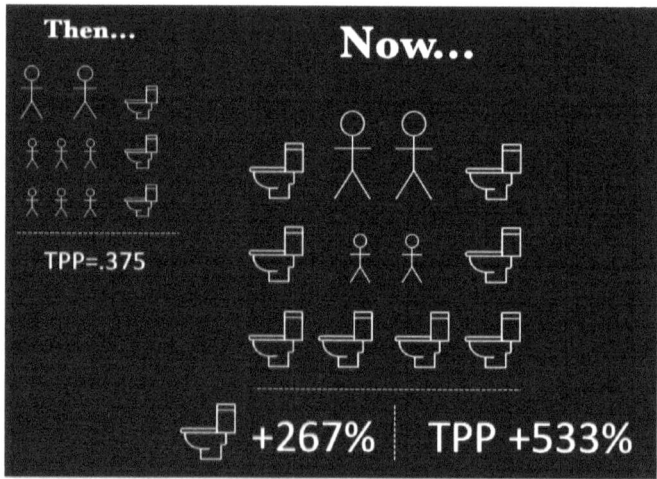

There's truth to the expression, "The things you own end up owning you," but it's not equally applicable to all purchases. Some of the things we've bought for our home provide significant value. Other things, less so. For example, I turned a storage room in our basement into a little gym that I use five times per week. That was a home run investment.

Our pool, on the other hand, is an under-utilized money pit. As the kids have gotten older, we swim less and less, but the monthly bills keep coming. I also lack the technical expertise to know if the pool guy is scamming me when he says, "The sand filter needs replacing because the O-ring is worn out." I hear this and think, "O-ring? Isn't that what brought down the space shuttle?" Then I fork over $800 or whatever it costs to replace a two-dollar piece of plastic.

Similarly, more toilets mean higher plumber bills, especially if your builder installed high-end German plumbing, for which replacement parts must be flown in First Class on Lufthansa.

To be clear, I am not whining about owning a big house or lamenting my own consumerist obsessions. I like stuff. But it's clear that most of us consume well past the point of "enough," and the housing market has evolved to enable this inclination. According to Census.org, the percentage of newly built U.S. homes with 2.5 bathrooms or more tripled from 1978 until 2016, and those with 3+ bathrooms almost quintupled. Americans love toilets!

Are there more people living in each home? No. In fact, average residents per household *decreased* during this time by 16%—from 3.01 to 2.54—while home size increased by 61%, to 2,687 square feet. So those dirty '70s hippies had 551 square feet each, while the average, clean 2015 person enjoyed 1,057 square feet.

I'm part of the problem. My parents' 2,251 square-foot home provided just over 280 square feet for each of its eight inhabitants (until my older siblings *finally* moved out). My current 6,450 square-foot home accommodates each of us with 1,612 square feet. But ours isn't even close to the biggest house in our neighborhood. Some dude down the street just built a 15,000-foot monster, which is rumored to have a 20-car garage in the basement to showcase his vintage Porsches and Ferraris. It makes our place look like a cute little cottage.

So what's the optimal home size? I don't know and the question is complicated by the fact that a house is a static structure while our needs are fluid. We bought this place when my kids were basically infants. Back then, I just wanted enough space so that I didn't have to take my shoes off as soon as I walked in the door for fear of waking a sleeping baby. That was absolutely the case in our previous home, a 1,500-square-foot Los Angeles bungalow.

Now that they're teenagers, I would happily trade interior space for a bigger yard in which we could kick the soccer ball around for however many fleeting evenings they might deign to do so. Before long, they'll both be out of high school and we will, presumably, be empty-nesters, banging around this big ol' lonely shell.

Since spatial requirements change over time, it would be a lot easier if houses were made of Play-Doh. You could just add a little space when you need it, then subtract as your needs decline. But that's not reality, so we just buy the most we can afford, stick with it for a certain number of years, and then make corrections during life's inflection points.

Despite anecdotal stories about van life and tiny homes, I don't see the trend toward bigger houses reversing any time soon. The pandemic drove sales of second homes to record levels, and I bet you can guess who succumbed to this instinct. That's right, yours truly is currently typing at 4,000 feet above sea level in our newly-built vacation place, surrounded by the Blue Ridge Mountains and seven additional toilets. What could possibly go wrong?

It's massively privileged but also totally absurd how, as we fulfill one desire, a new one creeps in. Not long ago, I was playing golf with a well-known comedian who grew up in a one-toilet house. After explaining my theory of bathroom opulence to him, I asked what his current TPP was.

"I don't know," he said, taking the cigar from his mouth, "Should I count the shitter on my plane?"

Money Isn't What You're Missing

What I've learned after years of studying money and happiness
MEDIUM, OCTOBER 2020

In the oft-quoted climax of the 1996 blockbuster *Jerry Maguire*, Tom Cruise stares through teary eyes at Renée Zellweger, the love interest he'd almost let slip through his distracted, metaphorical hands.

His last-chance pitch to win her back: "You complete me."

This sincere vulnerability captured her heart and five Oscar nominations despite—or perhaps because of—the fact that his revelation perpetuates a prevalent but childish fantasy: that each of us is an incomplete person, one element shy of perfection. But, if the universe would just grant us that missing thing, we could become our fully realized selves.

I remember watching this scene in the theater and thinking, "What a load of Hollywood fairy tale crap!" Yet in one area of my life, I applied Jerry's flawed logic: I thought money would complete me.

Ever since I was a boy, I dreamed of being rich. Part of this fixation came from a desire to avoid the financial stress I sensed in my parents as they raised us six children. Another part of me wanted the material things we didn't have, like a big house, fancy cars, and an Atari 2600. But most of all, I had mistakenly linked wealth with importance, and I believed that money would (cringe) "make me whole."

Fast forward a couple decades when, as an early employee of Facebook, I earned millions in the company's initial public offering. Thinking I had it made, I quit my job with no plan. I simply walked away from my career at age 42, figuring, "I'm rich—all my problems are solved!"

I could not have been more wrong. Since then, a big part of my life's work has been to explore what wealth means, how it changes us, how it leaves us the same. I'm not talking only to millionaires here. This message is for anyone who is breaking their neck trying to earn money at the expense of more meaningful things, like their relationships and doing their best work.

I'm not going to lie: the first three months of my new financial reality were fantastic. I took some great trips, exercised like crazy, and read many of the books that had been gathering dust on my nightstand. Most refreshingly, I lived those 90 days without the constant stress of sales quotas, office politics, and the zero-sum Darwinism of coach-class business travel.

But before long, I found myself feeling, well, lonely. I also developed the nauseating feeling that I had made a colossal mistake. Not only had I walked away from a lucrative job at an exciting company, I had also detached myself from the brilliant and funny colleagues who had kept me on my toes. Now, instead of working as part of a team to help solve our clients' problems, I filled my days refining my golf swing and grilling a lot of chicken. Unoccupied and omnipresent, I drove myself—and my wife—nuts.

One thing was certain: early retirement wasn't sexy or fulfilling. I didn't feel important, and I definitely didn't feel "complete." I had gotten everything I ever wanted, but I just felt like a rich loser. It was all very confusing.

So I searched for answers. I read dozens of books about wealth and happiness. I sought out wisdom from the Buddha, the Gospel, and The Suze Orman. I eventually synthesized the story of this quest in my podcast, on which I explore the connection between money and contentment with the top thinkers on the subject.

I began to see how the cognitive errors humans make with money were presenting themselves in my life. I learned about the hedonic treadmill, the process of mental adaptation by which we return to a base state of happiness after an exceptionally "good" event (like winning the lottery) or a very "bad" one (like losing one's legs in a car accident).

Despite this new knowledge, I still found myself thinking, "I'm not a lottery winner—I earned my money." One day, I stumbled upon a Credit Suisse white paper concluding that professionals who stop working post-windfall are often "blindsided by the resulting dislocation and feelings of loss and sadness and difficulty in finding new, fulfilling work."

Still, I thought, "I don't deserve to complain. I've got it made, right?"

Then I interviewed the author and financial therapist Brad Klontz, who works with ultra-high net worth clients. I asked him, somewhat facetiously, what billionaires could possibly have to worry about. He chuckled at my sarcasm, reminded me that the super-rich are still human beings, and added, "when you are already wealthy, and you are grappling with your own imperfections, you can't indulge in the fantasy that money will make everything better."

Said more simply, money won't fix you. *You* have to fix you. And until you disavow yourself of the notion that wealth (or six-pack abs, or Renée Zellweger) will make you feel "complete," you will be chasing a pipe dream. To be clear, I am not suggesting that money doesn't matter. It does. Solvency is glorious and a goal to which we should all commit ourselves. But stacking Benjamins up to the ceiling will not change how you feel when you look in the mirror.

It's comforting to attribute feelings of incompleteness to something we haven't yet attained. But as long as we do so, we avoid taking responsibility for the shortcomings that keep us from feeling like our best selves.

What most of us are missing isn't wealth, it's perspective. It's the acceptance that "completion" doesn't arrive when your checking account hits a specific number or when you win another's heart. Completion arrives when we accept the good things we already have going for us, and when we forgive ourselves for not being perfectly whole in the first place. That doesn't make for very quotable dialogue in Oscar-winning movies, but it does lead to a much more satisfying life.

The Streaming Services Cluster*ck

One man's attempt to impose order over an inconsequential part of his life.

SUBSTACK, SEPTEMBER 2023

"It's quite simple," I said to my wife and kids over dinner recently. "If you want to watch Amazon Prime, Starz, or AMC+, log into Amazon. To watch Disney+, Hulu, or ESPN+, go directly to those apps but use the Disney credentials. And use Roku if you want to watch Showtime, Paramount+, or Acorn TV, whatever that is."

"Acorn's my British murder show channel," my wife explained with a demonic grin. Then she asked, "But what about Apple TV+? They just released a new season of *The Morning Show*."

"Well, that's just Apple TV, which is its own thing, like Netflix and HBO Max, er, Max. But for whatever reason, we use *your* Apple log-in for that one."

Then my 14-year-old son spoke up, "Speaking of which, Mom, I tried to log in to Apple to watch Atlanta United on MLS Season Pass but I couldn't get in. Did you change your password?"

"I can't remember," she replied. "I'll look later."

"Where do we go to watch Peacock?" asked my 12-year-old daughter.

"Nowhere," I said. "We don't have Peacock."

My son immediately piped up, "Yeah we do."

"We do?" I asked.

"Yeah, I just watched a Premier League match on there the other day."

My daughter laughed and summed it all up for the table. "Dad is *so* confused."

She's got that right. Dad *is* confused. And if *you're* confused about what, whom, and how much you are paying for streaming services, you are not alone. At some point, the effort to combat this costly chaos is pointless. But I was just stupid enough to try.

Last week, Hulu sent me an email announcing an increase in our ad-free subscription rate from $14.99 to $18.99 per month. I asked myself, "Wait, don't we already get Hulu as part of the Disney+ bundle? Which led me to two questions: 1) why am I paying for it separately, and 2) where the hell did I sign up for it in the first place?" Answer: Roku. I think.

So, I went to Roku, where I did not see Disney+ but I did see my wife's English homicide network and a subscription to Paramount+. That's fine—hey, everybody loves *Yellowstone*—but I was pretty sure I was already paying for Paramount through Apple TV.

Yet upon logging onto said app, I found no P+ subscription listed. Was I misremembering? I checked my email Trash folder and there I saw receipts for Paramount from Apple every 30 days for the past 10 months. Good, I'm not crazy. But where in the hell do I manage that subscription?

A little further investigation and a lot of frustration revealed that we were paying for Paramount+ not through Apple TV+ but through my wife's Apple App Store account, along with a subscription for MGM+.

All these + sign channels, distributed through a variety of platforms, add up to one big shit show. It made me nostalgic for simpler times. Cutting the cord has indeed provided consumers with excellent content and the promised flexibility to customize channel subscriptions, but it's also generated boatloads of confusion. Say what you want about the pricing and forced bundles of old-school cable operators, customers got *one* easy-to-understand monthly bill from *one* provider each month.

Today, TV subscriptions are scattered about like plastic in the digital ocean. You buy your core, "over-the-top" TV from YouTube, Roku, Sling, Amazon, Hulu, or DirecTV, then add on your preferred mix of premium channel services. But—as far as I can tell—each of the TV providers provides some but not all of the premia, so you've got to cobble together a few here and a few there.

Figuring out who you're paying for what requires a full team of KPMG forensic accountants. Six bucks here, twelve bucks there—no one charge is a big deal but when you look at the total, it really adds up. This death by 1,000 digital cuts is driving me bonkers!

In the name of sanity, I resolved to streamline everything through as few providers as possible. As a first step, I went to YouTube TV, where we get our "TV-TV." And that's where I found our second Showtime subscription. Argghhh!

Okay, so I canceled those duplicate Hulu, Paramount, and Showtime subs. That felt good: $32 worth of post-tax money back in my pocket every month. This is totally worth the half-dozen hours of my life I've invested in this project so far.

Now back to the Disney networks. If I wasn't paying via Roku, where had I signed up? I checked our American Express statements going back a year. Apparently, I had purchased ESPN+ *a la carte*, but there was no record of any Disney transaction. So I went to DisneyPlus.com and clicked on my account settings where they informed me that I could manage my subscription at Verizon.com. Damn you, Bob Iger!

I vaguely remember getting that bundle as part of my cell phone service and it's a nice perk, but is it worth introducing an additional relationship into our home where the four of us have to stay on top of yet another user/PW, recurring charges, consolidations, constantly updated user agreements, etc.?

Of course, this raises the question of how many premium channels we really need. For some of the apps, you know what you're getting. I consider Netflix a must-buy, same for Max (btw, whose genius idea was it to throw out "HBO," i.e., the brand that invented premium television?), and I guess you need Acorn TV if you are an Anglophile who likes to watch people die. But $9.99/month for Starz—what the hell is on Starz?

Channel	Platform	Monthly	Annually	STATUS
Amazon Prime	Amazon		$ 139.00	
Audible annual	Amazon		$ 229.50	
Audible monthly	Apple app store	$ 15.99		CANCELLED
AMC+	Amazon	$ 8.99	$ 107.88	CANCELLED
Starz	Amazon	$ 9.99	$ 119.88	CANCELLED
Showtime	Roku	$ 10.99	$ 131.88	CANCELLED
AcornTV	Roku	$ 6.99	$ 83.88	
Paramount+ Essent	Roku	$ 5.99	$ 71.88	CANCELLED
Hulu	Hulu	$ 14.99	$ 179.88	CANCELLED
Disney+ Bundle	Verizon	$ -	$ -	
YT TV	YouTube	$ 72.99	$ 875.88	
Showtime	YouTube	$ 11.00	$ 132.00	CANCELLED
ESPN+	Paul Apple app store	$ 9.00	$ 109.00	CANCELLED
Paramount+	SBS Apple app store	$ 11.99	$ 109.00	CANCELLED
MLS Season Pass	Apple TV	$ 12.99	$ 155.88	CANCELLED
Apple TV+	Apple TV	$ 6.99	$ 83.88	CANCELLED
MGM+ / Epix		$ 5.99	$ 71.88	CANCELLED
HBO/Max	HBO/Max	$ 15.99	$ 191.88	
Peacock	???	????		
Netflix	Netflix	$ 19.99	$ 239.88	
TOTAL		$ 240.86	$ 3,033.06	

When engaged in the quixotic attempt to gain control over the unimportant, always use Excel.

And TV is just one category of subscription in our house. God knows how many times I'm paying for other recurring charges like Xbox Game Pass, Xbox Live, the *New York Times*, *Wall Street Journal*, Wondery podcasts, Audible, Scribd, Amazon Prime, Dropbox, Greenlight, Epic books, a couple of Substacks, etc.

It's a real problem, so of course there are new apps available that help you identify and minimize all the subscriptions you're paying for. Guess how you pay for this nifty service? That's right, through a monthly subscription.

So where did things end up in this game of premium-channel Whac-A-Mole? I believe that by canceling and consolidating subs then pre-paying annually instead of monthly, I carved out maybe $1,200/

year in savings, which ain't nothing. My fear is that, within a few months, we'll be right back where we started.

The only bright spot of the whole experience was learning that, for the past nine months, my children have been watching Peacock by logging on to my brother's account. Maybe his kids are enjoying British bloodshed on my wife's Acorn TV.

31 Flavors of Comcast (a one-act play)

Customer service at its finest
MEDIUM, OCTOBER 2018

INT. COMCAST ICE CREAM SHOP, AFTERNOON

CUSTOMER: One scoop of vanilla ice cream, please.

SERVER: Great. That will be $100.

CUSTOMER: Really? $100 seems like a lot for a small serving.

SERVER: If I'm hearing you right, you'd like to save some money on your ice cream service. Is that correct?

CUSTOMER: Yes.

SERVER: Then let me tell you about our new ice cream bundles. For $8, I can get you one scoop of vanilla ice cream plus five scoops of pistachio, all covered in a quart of strawberry drizzle.

CUSTOMER: $8 is still a little steep, but fine. And I'll just take the vanilla part, and you can keep all that other stuff, okay?

SERVER: Unfortunately, I can't separate out any one flavor because we serve it only after mixing all the ingredients in our proprietary Xfensive Blender.™

CUSTOMER: But I'm looking at plain, unadulterated vanilla ice cream *right there*. Why do you have to pollute it with all that other stuff in order to price it lower?

SERVER: Corporate wants you to get the best value.

CUSTOMER: That doesn't make any sense. Just charge me eight bucks for one scoop of vanilla and let me get on with my life.

SERVER: Sir, let me ask you a question, how will you be using your ice cream?

CUSTOMER: How am I going to use it? I'm going to put it in my mouth then swallow it.

SERVER: Ahh, you're what we call a Tier 2 user. I've got just the package for you: for only $34.95 I can give you a gallon of vanilla with a pound of chocolate sprinkles.

CUSTOMER: A gallon? I only want a single scoop.

SERVER: The minimum order size is a gallon. Otherwise, we can't waive the delivery fees and utensil rental charges.

CUSTOMER: Delivery and utensil rental? I'm going to carry it home and eat it with my own spoon.

SERVER: I'm afraid we can't allow you to use your own equipment.

CUSTOMER: Why not?

SERVER: It might degrade the quality of our ice cream.

CUSTOMER: I can't believe I'm having this conversation, but since there are no other ice cream shops anywhere around here, fine. One gallon. I'll make some room in the freezer. But I don't need the sprinkles.

SERVER: No sprinkles? How come? Everybody loves sprinkles.

CUSTOMER: I'm a purist. Sue me.

SERVER: It's no problem. I'll get you a gallon of vanilla and upgrade you to our "Sprinkles-free" package for $44.95.

CUSTOMER: You're going to charge me an additional $10 for not taking the sprinkles?

SERVER: Yes, and we'll need to extend your contract another 18 months.

CUSTOMER: Wait, what contract?

SERVER: The contract for daily delivery of sprinkles-free vanilla ice cream. Our technician will bring it to your house each day between 8:00 a.m. and 8:00 p.m. for the next three years.

CUSTOMER: A gallon of ice cream every day for three years? I have no idea what I'll be hungry for a year from now. Plus the landscape of the ice cream marketplace is shifting so fast that your product could be totally obsolete by then.

SERVER: Sir, I'm trying to exceed your expectations here. But I can't sell you just one scoop of ice cream.

CUSTOMER: Why not?

SERVER: Because we aren't in the single-serving business. We are in the Gelato-as-a-Service industry (GaaS). You know, the subscription economy and all that.

CUSTOMER: Gelato-as-a-Service? Why Gelato?

SERVER: Because "GaaS" has a nice ring to it, and "ICaaS" sounds too much like "ISIS."

CUSTOMER: So, it's 36 months or nothing?

SERVER: That's correct. Subscription businesses garner crazy high valuations.

CUSTOMER: This is nonsense. I'm out of here.

SERVER: Wait, my supervisor just approved one final package to offer you. I can give you one scoop of vanilla ice cream in a cup for $8.

CUSTOMER: Yes. Fine. That's all I wanted in the first place.

SERVER: But before I can serve you, I'll have to come to your house and kick your dog.

Adventures in Affluence: Dry Cleaning

How a nice gesture unsurfaced my latent conflict
SUBSTACK, DECEMBER 2023

I just made the last dry-cleaning run of 2023. It was quite a haul to carry—so much weight pulled on the wire hangers that I felt pain in my wrist. In the other hand, I clutched a gift from the owner of the business.

As I walked into the house, Stacey, my wife, thanked me for picking up the clothes and said, "What else do you have there?"

"Oh, this is the bottle of champagne the dry cleaner gave us as a holiday present."

"That is *so* nice!" She cheered.

"It's not nice," I replied. "The guy's obviously screwing us over."

Having dealt with my chronic grumpiness for 19 years, my wife shook her head and looked at me with her "for a relatively nice guy, you can be such an a-hole" expression. I've seen it before.

"Why are you like this?" she said. "It's a sweet gesture."

Of course, I regretted my words immediately. All I meant was that whenever someone buys you champagne, they are either trying to have sex with you, or they've already made love to your wallet, whether or not you actually noticed. In the case of Dry Cleaner Guy, I'm almost certain it was the latter, and thus was I holding 750 milliliters of Mumm Napa Brut Prestige NV.

But Stacey was right. The sparkly wine was a sincere and unnecessary token of gratitude. In a weird way though, his holiday kindness triggered me, making me wonder, how did I get to a place where my annual dry-cleaning bill merits a bottle of medium-low-end bubbles?

When I grew up, there was no dry cleaning in the Ollinger house. My father, a nuclear engineer, wore a jacket and tie to work—a post-Vietnam, PermaPress office casual vibe. My mother was the homemaker, which meant that in addition to her day job at the church, she cooked dinner for eight people, prepped my dad's work outfit (I know, I know—the Patriarchy!), and washed the kids' clothes. At some point during my freshman year, Mom—to her credit—resigned this last duty, leaving me with the choice of whether or not I wanted to iron my school uniform. Outsourcing this task was never discussed.

I didn't *have* to do it, as plenty of my classmates walked the halls of St. Pius X Catholic High School in wrinkly button-downs. But I was vain and chose to press my shirts, most of which were a 50/50 poly/cotton blend, so it wasn't terribly difficult.

I went to college with a distinctly more affluent crowd, but most kids attended class in tees or golf shirts. However, there was one guy in particular who stood out. Along with his creased Duck Head khakis and shiny Weejuns, this 6'4" hair-gelled athlete wore heavily starched, 100% cotton, pinpoint Brooks Brothers dress shirts that required professional care. Every single day.

I remember seeing him transport his weekly dry-cleaning bounty—a cape of cellophane billowing over his shoulder—as he strode from his red BMW to the dorm, like the bad guy from every 80s teen movie. To his credit, he was unapologetically well put together even if, at 19, he dressed like the 56-year-old lawyer he would someday become.

It eventually occurred to me that he was spending more to clean his clothes than I earned every month in my work-study job. I wasn't jealous so much as curious—a wide-eyed witness to the habits of the wealthy. "So that's something you can spend money on. Who knew?"

In my first year out of college, I earned a $25,000 salary at an office job that required literal white collars, so I bought the best shirts TJ Maxx had to offer and splurged $.89 per day to get them cleaned.

That was a huge luxury. But as with so many other things, as you get older and make more money, luxuries eventually become thoughtless needs. And this one has expanded to the point where, today, we're laundering things like cashmere throw blankets and linen napkins—items I never considered owning, let alone paying to wash.

We arrived at this unconscious habit accidentally. I don't recall ever checking my dry-cleaning receipts in the past decade, and that $.89 per shirt is now probably $4. Maybe more. I have no idea because I never gave it any thought…until dude hit me with the bottle of bubbly and uncovered my latent dry-cleaning trauma, which I projected onto him.

Was it guilt or shame? Do I feel unworthy? Have I lost touch with who I used to be, or am I worried that my parents would consider me wasteful? Am I now the villain from the 80s movie, albeit balder and heavier?

I don't know, but I just checked my 2023 American Express account. This year's dry-cleaning expenditures totaled $1,773.86.

Damn. That's a lot. Next year, I expect Dom Perignon.

We Are All Phil Mickelson

All the moralizing about the Saudi golf league
reflects our collective self-deception
SUBSTACK, JUNE 2022

In his 1999 comedy special, *Bigger & Blacker*, Chris Rock makes a bold assertion about men and marital fidelity: "A man is basically as faithful as his options." Unattractive men lack any basis for claiming they would never commit adultery, says Rock, because nobody's trying to, ahem, make love to them. Though that's not how he phrases it.

I've been thinking about this theory recently as I've read the moralistic commentary about golfer Phil Mickelson's defection from the PGA Tour to LIV Golf, a new league backed by Saudi Arabia's sovereign wealth fund. LIV has reportedly guaranteed the six-time major tournament winner $200 million and offered lower-profile golfers tens of millions to play on their nascent tour. Those who accept the deal will earn a lot more money for playing fewer events—but will also be providing their tacit endorsement to the oppressive regime that has one of the worst human rights records on the planet, including the murder of journalist Jamal Khashoggi.

I've read a couple dozen pieces on the topic, but none exceeded the sanctimony of Sally Jenkins in the *Washington Post*. In "Golf has done so very much good—for Phil Mickelson and his pals," Jenkins tees off on Mickelson's greed, self-deception, and willingness to engage in sports-washing, a concept with which she should be very familiar, considering she co-authored two of Lance Armstrong's autobiographies.

While it's tempting to admonish the author for her own hypocrisy, I think it's more useful to use it as a lens through which to examine the bigger question: who among us would say "no" when a very desirable someone wants to fornicate with us or an evil institution offers to pay us an unfathomable amount of money to do the thing we love the most?

Phil's dilemma is very distinct and high-profile, but each of us—consciously or unconsciously—commits numerous ethical compromises every day. Jenkins writes for a paper owned by Jeff Bezos, founder and executive chairman of Amazon. With only the slightest effort, she could identify numerous examples of the online retailing giant's practices that conflict with her stated principles, not limited to the fact that it serves Saudi consumers.

I am every bit as guilty of willful ignorance as anyone else. I read Jenkins' article on my iPhone, which was probably assembled in China and definitely contains cobalt, a metallic element that comes from the Congo, where it is dug manually—sometimes by children—out of the ground at god knows what ecological and human cost. While reading, I sipped a Diet Coke, which is also available on the baking streets of Riyadh.

When you stop to think about these questions, it makes you wonder. Is it wrong for Coca-Cola to provide refreshments to the average Saudi? Does my consumption of a company's product imply that I agree with every one of their current business practices or historical decisions? Think about automotive manufacturers. Spend five minutes googling Mercedes, Porsche, Toyota, or Mazda, and you learn that they have spent meaningful time on the "wrong side of history" (as determined by the winner). Speaking of cars, about 5% of the fuel in my tank is Saudi petrol, which may or may not be worse than gas refined from Russian or Venezuelan crude.

It was too much to consider while I sat on my couch, enjoying the final round of the RBC Canadian Open produced by The PGA Tour, which is now positioning itself as the ethical alternative to LIV. I was so engrossed in the birdies and eagles that I almost forgot to ask myself how the sponsor, Royal Bank of Canada, makes its money. A little querying unearthed the bank's participation in the IPO of Saudi Aramco—but doing business in the kingdom hardly makes them unique among the PGA's Official Partners. Indeed, Rolex, Chase, Lexmark, Pepsi, and KPMG also earn profits there.

So who's walking around pro golf with clean hands? Certainly not Rory McIlroy, last week's winner, who remains one of the top PGA holdouts. Maybe Rory (for the record, one of my favorite players) knows to steer clear after his five-year endorsement of Jumeirah, a super-luxury hospitality brand owned by Dubai Holdings, the investment fund of Sheikh Mohammed bin Rashid Al Maktoum, whom Wikipedia describes as "the ruler of Dubai."

Dubai may have a super neat indoor ski mountain, but Amnesty International reports the government also commits "serious human rights violations, including arbitrary detention, cruel and inhuman treatment of detainees…and violation of the right of privacy."

So give me a break on the "Phil's evil and the PGA Tour is pure" narrative. While there's no justifying Saudi human rights records, this isn't about golf's "integrity." It's about protecting the league and its massive revenues.

We all want to do the right thing, but truly steering clear of Saudi influence would mean not flying British Airways, riding in a Lyft, or staying in a Marriott, Hyatt, or Fairmont hotel. It would also require not owning stock—even if only through mutual funds—in Boeing, Raytheon, General Dynamics, or any other company that, with the consent of the U.S. government, sells weapons to the unsavory Gulf state. Do you know the names of every single stock held in your 401k? I don't.

I'm not sure it's possible to unravel this bowl of ethical spaghetti. These companies, their investors, host countries, suppliers, and customers are so intertwined that it seems impossible to disentangle. One thing is for sure: running a global business is not a black-and-white issue, and anyone who represents it that way isn't paying attention.

What ultimately happens with LIV should depend on the quality of competition. I suspect most golf fans will find the new events less interesting than what we're used to, and I hope we end up with a reunified and re-invigorated PGA Tour. But LIV should be given a chance to succeed on the merits of its product and not relative to the contrived moral superiority of the incumbent league.

Whether we admit it or not, we all dance with the devil. I do it. Sally Jenkins does it. The PGA Tour does it. How guilty we are depends on two things: 1) How honest we are with ourselves; and 2) Whether or not anyone actually wants to get naked with us.

We are all Phil Mickelson. He's just got more options.

WORK

Dare to Suck

Letting go of proficiency is the first step in the pursuit of mastery
SUBSTACK MAY 2023

"If you want to improve, be content to be thought foolish and stupid."
—*Epictetus*

The t-shirt read "Dare to Suck."

I was sitting in my first day of *Intro to Sitcom Acting* at Lesly Kahn and Co., a well-known acting school in Los Angeles, where my instructor had just handed me a pre-shrunk welcome gift.

Considering the provocative command, I asked, "Why in the world would you tell someone that they should suck?"

The instructor, a working TV actor with more than a decade in Hollywood, had seen plenty of new students cycle through this classroom, so he knew how to handle the new cohort's resident smart-ass.

"Lesly's not saying that you *should* suck," he replied. "She's saying that you *do* suck—at acting—now, but that you are here to suck less through study and hard work."

This was in 2006, during my first stint chasing comedy full-time. A lot has happened since then, and I outgrew the t-shirt long ago, but the words "Dare to Suck" have always stuck with me. When I re-committed myself to stand-up and writing 12 years ago, I became fully aware of what living the DTS motto really means. The scary truth about any new pursuit or reinvention—artistic, athletic, or commercial—is that success lies on a distant shore, across a perilous ocean of struggle. If you want to "make it," you must embrace the suck.

Mastery is a big deal for humans. Being really good at something creates a sense of well-being and purpose. It provides status, pride, a place in the world, and—sometimes—a source of income. Once attained, it is a great source of comfort.

So you'd think that an author writing about self-development would encourage his readers to figure out what they're great at. But, in his best-seller *The Subtle Art of Not Giving a F*ck*, author Mark Manson does the opposite, asking "What *pain* do you want in your life? What are you willing to struggle for?"

The first time I read this, my reaction was similar to my confusion over the DTS t-shirt. But like Lesly's, Manson's non-obvious advice makes perfect sense.

Mastery happens only after we invest the time and effort to get good at something (this is Malcolm Gladwell's "10,000 hour rule"). But practice means struggle, and because struggling is hard, we avoid tasks that don't mean that much to us. Manson challenges us to identify the thing we care about sufficiently to suck at, and struggle with, long enough to master.

Consider what it takes to learn a language. For a long time, I harbored the dream that, someday, I would learn to really speak Spanish, which I had studied in high school and college. Eight years ago, after six months of using Duolingo to refresh my vocabulary, I stepped up and enrolled in *una clase de Español*. I picked up a lot pretty quickly, but only a few sessions in, I remembered why I had quit the language after *Spanish 201*: because it's hard.

I had envisioned chatting with Messi after a match in Miami and delighting strangers with my bilingualism, but I didn't contemplate—nor was I committed to enduring—years of talking like a moronic pre-kindergartner until I broke through to fluency.

Manson contends that "Who you are is defined by what you're willing to struggle for," and this was an excellent example of that. My unwillingness to tolerate the discomfort of speaking ineloquently revealed that the goal just wasn't that important to me. In the beloved words of a former colleague, "the juice wasn't worth the squeeze."

Comedy, however, was another matter—boy was I willing to suck at that. I recently re-watched a video of my very first live comedy performance. It made me cringe. While there were some clever lines in there, it was hard to watch someone so new and unskilled at comedy (I kept my hand on my hip for the entire set!). But I was so protected by determination and self-delusion that I persisted and improved.

That's how you know. If you're crawling over the broken glass of imperfection and you still find yourself thinking, "this is worth doing," then that's your thing. Your mission from there is to embrace the pain and keep going.

So dare to suck. Dare to fail. Dare to make no money. Dare to have no outward signs of progress. Dare to get rejected by gatekeepers over and over. And over. Keep daring, keep sucking, and keep getting better, bit by barely perceptible bit, until one day, the shores of proficiency appear on the horizon.

Sucking will set you free, but you have to want to do it. If you're not willing to suck, your dream isn't a dream—it's a fantasy. Do something else.

The Pandemic Proved That Work Is a Privilege

I'm finally ready to start treating it that way
MEDIUM, MAY 2021

In early 2020, my fledgling stand-up comedy career was finally finding its footing. I had headlined Carolines on Broadway, was starting to work the road, and had meetings set in New York City with influential industry gatekeepers scheduled on March 17, about the time things got really crazy with Covid.

Of course, that NYC trip never happened. But lockdown did, and the momentum born from seven years of full-time grinding, open mics, and doing all possible gigs went straight down the toilet. I was scared and pissed off. But after a week or so, I realized something—all the clubs were closed, so no one was working. In this ultra-competitive industry, I wasn't losing any professional ground. Petty though it was, the rationalization soothed me.

The shutdown also freed me from the constant stress of emailing club bookers, networking for gigs with other comics, and posturing on social media about the quality and quantity of my upcoming shows. I would never have chosen it, but when work stopped, so ceased the FOMO, the constant hustle, and the weight of career comparison that went with it. Like Elsa in *Frozen*, I let it go.

Whether we admit it or not, there were some positive elements about life in quarantine. Obviously, millions lost jobs and loved ones, students lost the on-campus experience, and parents—especially mothers—had to juggle work, homeschooling, and self-care. But for a lot of us who didn't experience tragedy, the shutdown provided much-needed decompression. Now that we're coming out of it, quarantine is also providing perspective into how we feel about our "normal" selves.

In many ways, the pandemic pace was better, and I don't just mean "better for introverts," as many reported. I mean that forcing hard-charging, extroverted people to sit their ambitious, loud-talking butts down and take a break was good for us. We adapted to a slower pace by cooking every night. We did puzzles and played video games with the kids. We went to parks, rode bikes, and changed the definition of success from "constantly moving forward" to "constructively getting through the day."

Now that our lives consist of a new version of our old routines, it's tempting to say, "I'll never go back to the success-obsessed person I was." But I know I will. Not only because it's in my nature, but because Covid reminded me of something we should never forget: work—however you define it—is a privilege.

Covid taught me many lessons, including "you're not entirely in control of your life," "our healthcare system is held together by Silly Putty," and "you're one global crisis away from sweatpants being your default clothing choice." But it was also a stark reminder that our brief lives contain only so many summers, hump days, and March 17ths. So we should make the most of them.

That's why Old Me got his shots and is reawakening like an athlete recovering from injury, eager to get back on the field and play. Covid makes me want to write more, to write more honestly, and to perform with my viscera dangling for all to see. I'm saying "yes" to non-traditional opportunities because I want to leave it all out there.

Maybe I'll regain the momentum I once had. Perhaps I won't. But the point is to try. To work toward something. To gather rosebuds, to *carpe* that *diem*, and grow through the struggle to improve and to accumulate experiences on the road to my truth while I am still able to do so.

I'm sure many do not share my enthusiasm about going back to work. There might be a lesson in this. If you are someone who stopped doing your thing for a year, and you aren't chomping at the bit to get back to it, that should tell you something about your commitment. Maybe the literal and metaphorical spring of 2020 can be your motivation to plant some new seeds, plot out your limited days ahead.

Covid demonstrated that we can never be sure what life has in store for us. There always seems to be a war looming these days, another pandemic is waiting in the wings, and economic recession is bound to return before too long. What's 100% certain is that—at some point in the not-too-distant future—all of us will be forced to slow down again, this time due to the more personal crisis of age and declining health. At that point, no vaccination will give us another opportunity to get after our passions. It's now or never.

There was a comfort to Covid. The permission to take it easy for a while put life in perspective. I know now that I can have a meaningful life outside of my professional identity, and I'll be okay, whether or not I ever "make it." But while you have the chance, why not give it everything you've got?

Gary v. Jerry

Why Gary Gulman resents rich people
SUBSTACK, JANUARY 2024

If I could choose a super-power—after X-ray vision and the ability to fly—I would choose the ability to implant in other people a faith that they can achieve and enjoy financial prosperity. Lacking this trust in economic self-determination, a person will never reach his or her full potential.

A prime example of the kind of attitude that limits financial success and fulfillment is seen in *Born on Third Base*, the recent Max—fka "HBO"—comedy special by the transcendentally talented Gary Gulman. *New York Times* comedy critic Jason Zinoman called it a "meticulously funny hour that digs into the gap between the haves and have-nots." That it is, but as someone who has been both a "have" and "have not," and who has performed thousands of stand-up comedy shows across the country, I feel strong but conflicting emotions about Gary's message, which the fawning crowd receives well, but is nevertheless born of resentment.

I grew up one of six children to parents who were scarred by the Depression and never made a lot of money. We had all we needed, but budgetary stress lingered like an irritating, omnipresent guest. I channeled that angst toward building a great corporate career, and found one that even allowed me to retire early.

Gary Gulman was born a "have not" and eventually became one of the most gifted comedians on the planet. A dedicated craftsman, he weaves jokes, observations, and wordplay into intricate tapestries of humor. His bits about non-obvious topics—grapes versus grapefruit, the origin of the 50 state abbreviations, and Hitler's "shenanigans"—have earned him a spot in the pantheon of modern, cerebral comedy.

Born on Third Base is a worthy addition to his body of work. Always vulnerable about his insecurities and struggles with mental health, Gary reflects on his impoverished youth and the indignity of free school lunch (and breakfast!). He calls bullshit on the welfare-dependency trope and makes a compelling argument that no one understands the zero-sum realities of home economics like poor kids. However, he also demonstrates a crippling poverty mindset and a crushing envy of those who have more than he does.

He's discussed this issue before. In his 2023 memoir, *Misfit*, Gary writes at length about his grudge against wealthy people, quoting *The Great Gatsby*: "I have never been able to forgive the rich for being rich, and it's colored my entire life and work." He goes on to explain how much he hates elitist "sports" like skiing and how he sees the resulting torn ACLs and broken limbs as "cosmic judgement for their opulent f-you to the working class."

One sees this rancor coloring his work in the new special when he analyzes, as he calls it, the "cartoonish" income inequality between him and Jerry Seinfeld. In this "Jerry v. Gary" bit, he suggests with numerical precision that, since the two men are in the same business, there could be no justifiable reason that Jerry is a billionaire while Gary's net worth hovers around $89,000. He wonders how it could possibly be fair that Jerry owns a building to house his Porsche collection when Gary and his wife can't afford a 4-slice toaster.

As funny as this juxtaposition is, the logical—and perhaps, factual—errors run deep. First, Jerry's astronomical net worth came not from joke-telling, but from television production. If Gary wishes to close the gap between Jerry and himself, all he has to do is go back in time and co-create a sitcom so popular that 76 million people watch the finale. He could then sit back for 25 years and watch his net worth soar, propelled by re-runs, residuals, and compound interest.

But very few comedians have created such beloved touchstones of pop culture. Ray Romano probably came closest by starring in *Everybody Loves Raymond* and earning himself hundreds of millions, which is a lot, but still only a fraction of Jerry's balance sheet.

Ray doesn't seem bothered by this disparity, but Gary really takes it personally. Why? Has Jerry's success deprived Gary of a single dollar? Of course not. In fact, one could argue that the former paved the way for the latter by proving the market for nuanced observational comedy and helping to keep open the clubs where Gary eventually learned his craft.

On the subject of craft, one explanation for the two comics' divergent monetary outcomes lies with their respective products. In the his new special, Gary alleges that he is a better comedian than Jerry. That may or may not be true, but guess what—it doesn't matter. While brilliance and economic success are likely correlated, massive financial windfalls in entertainment result only from mass appeal. And while Gary ostensibly speaks on behalf of the common man, he requires the crowd to meet him at intellectual heights well above that of mainstream "brutes," as he acknowledges in *Misfit*. His jokes are too clever, dare I say precious—yes, I dare—for a mass audience. And for better or worse, that's where the money is.

There are a million examples of this problem, in every art form. Short stories author George Saunders might be the most talented writer alive, but he'll never earn as much money as the person who composes the next *Avengers* script. Taylor Swift may not be the best guitarist in the world, but right now, she is the most popular, and that's why she, like the guy who played "Jerry" on *Seinfeld*, is a billionaire.

On the surface, Gary is calling out inequality, but by creating this "us vs. them" duality, he's just perpetuating the paralyzing attitudes that will keep him and millions who share his resentment from achieving their financial potential.

Here's another example of his flawed thinking: Gary contends that growing up poor makes a person more empathetic, offering as proof the way upper-class customers "wag their finger" at Chipotle or Subway employees. While I have no doubt many affluent people act entitled in public, whenever I see a viral video of a Burger King brawl or Waffle House fight club that started because the cashier didn't provide extra napkins, the fist-swinging, hair-pulling customers don't appear to be doctors, lawyers, or hedge fund managers. He's right that the treatment of service workers is an issue of class, but only in the sense that "class" is defined by the way someone, rich or poor, demonstrates courtesy to their fellow human.

The most intriguing part about Gary's situation is that he almost certainly earns over $1 million per year. If, for example, he sells out his upcoming show at Washington D.C.'s 1,800-seat Warner Theater for a very conservative average of $75/ticket, his 50% of the gross would total about $68k. Deduct 25% for agents, managers, and travel, and he would still take home $50,000 for the evening. That buys a lot of toasters.

One million annual dollars isn't a billion in net worth, but it places him deep into the top 1% of U.S. earners, which is where things get complicated. Gary's economic reality is now at odds with his self-image and long-held animus. As a person already scarred by childhood deprivation, this cognitive dissonance induces in him yet more guilt and shame. To atone for the perceived sin of his accomplishment, he projects that transgression onto someone who has even more. In the process, he transmits the virus of self-limiting resentment onto a delighted audience that has no idea—or, worse, just doesn't care—that they're infected.

Gary's comedy has given me a lot of joy over the years and he has earned all of his artistic and financial success. I wish I could give him the power to enjoy it. Because welfare might not keep people poor, but negative beliefs sure do.

Why Comedy Clubs Matter

Thoughts on the closing of Carolines on Broadway
SUBSTACK, DECEMBER, 2022

After 40 years of presenting the most famous and promising comedians on the planet, the legendary club, Carolines on Broadway, closed on January 1, 2022.

In a world with too many comics and not enough mics, the loss of an iconic stage is always a blow to the comedy community. And Carolines will always be special to me because, in 2019, the club named me to their Breakout Artist Series. That recognition meant a lot to my career, but it's not the main reason this iconic room holds a dear place in my heart.

Carolines matters to me personally because one Saturday in October 2004—even before I committed full-time to a comedy career—I went to see a friend's show there. I was alone, so the hostess seated me with my buddy's wife and her friends. Also at our table, a few seats down from me, was a striking brunette who—at the moment I write this—is sleeping in the master bedroom of the cozy home we share with our 13-year-old daughter and 14-year-old son.

That's right, though she swears she doesn't remember meeting me that day, my wife Stacey and I began our relationship with a chance encounter in the Carolines showroom. Our loving marriage has endured 15 years and produced two cherished human beings. It all started because Caroline Hirsch and her partner risked their money and reputations to create a space for people to gather, laugh, and—perhaps—make babies.

When people shit on capitalism, they probably aren't thinking about a young woman who invested her savings and four subsequent decades of work into a place where—literally—millions of people have spent a small and sometimes consequential part of their lives. But that's what Caroline did, and it resulted in more than just a successful business.

According to a 2018 *Forbes* article, the club sold about 8,500 tickets per month. That translates to over 100,000 butts in seats every year—butts that brought with them hearts and souls, souls getting a break from the grind of their job, hearts forgetting about the troubles at home, or the simple elevation of someone's day in the communion of laughter.

Comedy clubs obviously create lots of jobs for their employees and a lot of opportunities for comedians to perform, grow, and earn a living. But the best ones understand that their business is way more than providing yucks in order to sell mountains of cheese sticks and oceans of draft beer.

Like Carolines, clubs such as QED in Astoria, Zanies in Nashville, The Laughing Skull in Atlanta, the Hollywood Improv, and a bunch of others around the country, understand that every comedy show is a unique combination of ever-changing variables. The inimitable blend of the day's news cycle, the temperature in the room, the new material attempted by the host, and the respective mindsets of the two, 200, or 2,000 audience members has never existed before, and will never be repeated.

The club's management curates the space and the performers with the goal of nurturing the shared, transcendent human experience that only live performing arts provide. At their core, these clubs share one common ideal: that comedy, as a medium for human bonding, is sacred.

If we learned nothing else from quarantining during Covid, it is that being together, in person, nourishes our well-being. But the spaces where we gather don't happen by accident. Comedy clubs exist because someone with vision took a risk and worked like hell to put on great shows, night after night after night. Most of the time, these shows result in a fun evening of laughter. Other times, they spawn brand new families.

Carolines closing is a huge drag, but it reminds me to be grateful and stay present in the moment. All of this stuff around us—our institutions, our comedy shows, our health, and today's weather—are temporary. The fact that we are here at all is a tremendous privilege that we should never forget.

So thank you, Caroline and your team, for creating a venue where laughs were shared and new lives began. Carpe Diem.

How to Host a Traveling Comedian

I won't stay for free with just anybody…

SUBSTACK, JULY 2022

Great news, friend—I'm doing comedy in your town next month. What's that? Oh sure, I'd love to stay at your place. Thanks for the offer!

Sometimes clubs put me up in a hotel or condo, but I'm coming to a festival that doesn't provide lodging. I actually like it better like this. If I got a room in some hotel, you and I'd have dinner one night and then go our separate ways. Now, I'll have the chance to get to know your second wife while I eat Honey Nut Cheerios in my pajamas at noon at your kitchen table. If she's like my other buddies' new brides, she might not realize how close we were 25 years ago and will ask more than once, "How long will you be staying?"

This is an excellent question because I really don't know. If I do well in the early rounds, I'll have more spots next week. It's probably best to leave things open-ended.

I realize that hosting an out-of-towner in your spare bedroom or basement might be inconvenient, especially for the kids, whose personal space I will occupy. But they'll come around when they learn that your house guest/former fraternity brother has appeared on The Weather Channel, the TV Guide Channel, and once "shared the stage" with Jeff Dunham. Don't worry—I haven't let success go to my head.

You're probably wondering if I have any dietary restrictions. I do not. Just stock the kitchen with a broad selection of healthy entrees, fruits, vegetables, and low-sugar almond milk, please. And if cookies from your local bakery happen to show up, I won't complain. (For real, buy some cookies.)

But don't go to any trouble. Just ask your house manager to take care of it. You do have a house manager, don't you?

I'll want to unwind when I get home from shows well after midnight—don't worry if your dog starts barking; I'm pretty chill about that kind of thing. I will have eaten earlier, but a nightcap of olives, artisanal cheeses, and a bottle of red would be dynamite—nothing fancy—maybe a California cabernet that retails for around $40. Come to think of it, let's not quibble over a few bucks—get the $50 bottle.

I won't want to make any noise cleaning up after I eat, so I'll just leave the dirty dishes on the counter. Speaking of which, I know I shouldn't smoke in the house, so I will put my cigarette butts in your favorite coffee mug and set it on top of your Big Green Egg.

Since I'm staying with you, you'll definitely want to come see me perform! I'll have as few as one but as many as five shows, all of which will require you to purchase a full-priced ticket and get a babysitter. Here's a link to the club/brewery/coffee shop's website—don't forget to share it with all of your friends, as seats are definitely available.

By the way, where do you keep the club soda? I may have spilled coffee on that white rug in your living room. It looks like it's pretty new. Is it new? Also, do we have any more coffee?

I perform in the evenings, so I'm free all day. Let's play golf at your country club! Oh, I forgot, you don't belong to one. Can you call one of your friends and score me a tee time? No, not at that club—get me on the one that's more exclusive. They'll love hosting me, as I'll tell them jokes on every single tee box and green.

With regard to that material, please don't call me out when I'm running bits but pretend to be answering your question about how life is going. It's going great. But you know what I need more than a Netflix half-hour special? Health insurance!

Ha ha.

Well, thanks for letting me stay with you, bro. I'm sorry your work schedule, doctor's appointments, and parent-teacher meetings prevented us from hanging out more than we did. The good news is that I crushed the festival and "won" the chance to host a weekend at the local club next month.

    Cool if I crash again?

Dear Podcast Publicist…

Your spraying and praying isn't helping you
MEDIUM, JANUARY 2022

Dear Podcast Publicist,

Thanks for your email. Before I reply to the enticing proposition to interview your creepy client with dubious credibility in his purported field of expertise, allow me to acknowledge the necessary and critical symbiosis between publicists and media properties.

Journalists, TV producers, and—yes—independent podcasters require alluring, intelligent guests to create compelling content. When you connect us with a great interview, it's a win-win, so we're happy to consider pitches that are frequently off the mark. But after three years of studying incoming inquiries, I can testify that your strategy of slinging thousands of emails against the wall and hoping some of them stick is working against you.

The first problem is that "spraying and praying" will only land interviews on crappy shows lacking rigorous booking guidelines. Podcasts with vision proactively maintain qualitative and topical standards that help them rise to the top, if only to their loyal listeners' queue. We *seek out* excellence. We do not wait until adequate conversational partners arrive in our Inbox.

In hundreds of original episodes of my podcast, I have hosted a total of seven interviewees from in-bound publicity inquiries. That's only 5%, and all were homerun guests, including a famous musician who has sold over 20 million records, a podcaster who reaches 19 million listeners per month, and an international best-selling author who has sold over 8 million books.

Not coincidentally, I have booked zero guests who offer:

- A "sure-fire methodology to earn money in real estate while you sleep"
- "10% off their new, online day-trading course"
- The only "proprietary, bro-tastic formula to make you a millionaire before you turn 30!"

I get it; you have a job to do. And I recognize that my little podcast doesn't generate Joe Rogan-ish numbers or *Smartless*-esque celebrity cred. I know I'm not going to be the first pitch for Oprah's new book, so I keep an open mind. This is why I still read every one of the dozens of weekly pitches I get, which fall into roughly two categories:

1. Those representing high-quality, legitimate authors, broadcasters, directors, or creatives promoting a new project.
2. Those representing any human with a pulse and a PR budget pitching God-knows-what self-help, get-rich-quick nonsense.

When I see emails from Random House, HarperCollins, HBO, or Netflix, I am eager to open them and learn what's on the other side. Even if it's not a fit, I know the note will be professional, well-written, and thoughtfully positioned. When I see emails from "PodcastBlasters," "GetBOOKEDonPodcasts," or "PodcastGuests4Free," I think, "this is going a total waste of time." I am rarely surprised.

If this perspective sounds snobby, I came to it honestly—by reviewing thousands of pitches and seeing the same amateur tactics repeated ad nauseum. So if you want to move up from the schlocky crowd, into that first bucket of trusted publicists, keep the following in mind:

- **Be choosy about who you represent.** The people you pitch are your brand. It's that simple. When you represent digital snake-oil sales folk, their slimy sheen rubs off on you. If economic necessity requires you to take on a shady client, practice restraint in your pitching.

- **Less Is More.** The more crap you send me, the less credibility your future emails carry. If you want your client to stand out, refrain from the automated "I enjoyed your recent episode with [fill-in-the-blank-name]." It's transparently insincere. Invest the time to learn what each podcaster is looking for. Yes, it takes longer, but it will yield a much higher hit rate than your current practices.
- **Please don't review my podcast unless you've actually listened to it and honestly like it.** This tactic was eye-catching at first but now it's just irritating. No review at all is better than an inauthentic one. If you have *for real listened* and *do find it compelling*, make that clear in the first or second sentence. I will send you a tote bag.
- **Every time you follow up, an angel loses its wings.** For the love of all things holy, do not send follow-up emails. "Just checking in about the below" or "wanted to bump this to the top of your Inbox," tells me you do not respect my time. I would actually love to send a thoughtful reply to every inquiry but producing a good podcast consumes so much time that there is none left for professional niceties. If you don't get a reply, assume it's a "no thank you."

All this is a long way of saying, I will pass on this week's pitch but I do want to hear from you in the future *if* you have a high-quality client who is relevant to my show's theme. Learning that requires you to exert extra care and attention to your pitches.

But don't do it for me. Do it for yourself and the redemption of your spammy soul.

Love,
Podcasters Everywhere

The Thing Malcolm Gladwell Forgot to Mention

Why 10,000 hours doesn't guarantee the success of your dream
MEDIUM, MARCH 2021

In his 2008 bestselling book Outliers, Malcolm Gladwell delivered to the mainstream the theory that gaining mastery of any craft requires 10,000 hours of dedicated practice—as he calls it, "the magic number of greatness."

The trade you're in doesn't matter much, he argued, because what all skill-based pursuits have in common is that repetition on a massive scale is the only path to proficiency. Similarly, the actual number of hours may vary, but that's not the point. In this controversial model, "10,000 hours" plays the same symbolic role as "40 years in the desert" did for the Israelites: a long, arduous journey through a wilderness beset with strife and dream-killing doubt.

But while Gladwell is right that even the most naturally gifted cannot succeed without putting in the time, his maxim lacks a crucial caveat: 10,000 hours of sincere, focused training in a craft is just the price of admission. You can put in the time and still suck.

Okay, perhaps that's an oversimplification. If you practice at something 40 hours a week for five years (40 hrs/week * 50 weeks/year * five years = 10,000 hours), you will definitely improve and might even become a master. But mastery of a thing doesn't guarantee "success" in the form of extrinsic rewards—that is, money, fame, respect, or even a job. You could be the best oboe player in North America but still not be able to pay your bills or have your brilliance acknowledged by the world. And when you are really, really good at something but no one notices, it feels like sucking.

The mistake lies in the logic of our dreams. (How about?: "This situation arises from the logic of our collective dreams.") When most people envision the perfect way to make a living, they think of activities that 1) are fun; 2) provide accolades; and 3) don't require long division. This general passion for the glittery, self-aggrandizing, and nonquantitative results in a supply of pretty good comedians, okay singer-songwriters, and decent essay writers (hi there!) that significantly exceeds the demand for our services—which means that almost none of us will be able to earn a living solely by "doing our thing."

Morgan Housel, the financial writer and author of *The Psychology of Money*, captured this stark reality in a recent blog post: "Being good at something doesn't promise rewards. It doesn't even promise a compliment. What's rewarded in the world is scarcity, so what matters is what you can do that other people are bad at."

Housel's declaration here is the sobering, no-bullshit side of the 10,000 hours coin: the marketplace doesn't care how much you practice. It cares very little about how good you've gotten. And it definitely doesn't care how much you care. Either someone else can't live without what you have to offer, or your dream is a hobby.

This, of course, isn't the way things *should* be. Anyone who loves to bake and puts in the time *should* be able to earn lots of money selling muffins. Novelists who can weave language into a tapestry of emotions *should* get more respect than TikTok celebrities who attract millions by lighting their farts on camera. My Donna Summer tribute band *should* be on the next cover of *Rolling Stone*.

But that's not how the world works. So before you quit your job to master the oboe, develop the next smash video game, or disrupt the grilled cheese industry with your networked panini app, check your motivations and consider a line from "Wishing Well," a song by alternative rocker Bob Mould: "There's a price to pay for a wish to come true—trade a small piece of your life."

When you commit to spending 10,000 hours getting good at something, you are trading a *big* piece of your life, and the only thing you are guaranteed is learning the answer to the question, "What would happen if I gave it my all?" That's it. Trying is your trophy, and everything else—if there is anything else—is gravy.

The good news is that no matter what else happens, persistence will generate meaningful intrinsic rewards. If you keep going down the 10,000 hours path, you will experience the joy of engaging in your art, the pride that comes from hard-won improvement, and the camaraderie you feel when you find fellow travelers who share your passion.

So let go of external outcomes and do your thing for the love of the craft. Love is not just the only sensible reason to chase a dream. It's also the fuel that will keep you practicing while the world ignores you.

The Best Worst Interview Advice Ever

How to avoid a catastrophic meeting
LINKEDIN, MAY 2018

During the dot-com meltdown of 2001, my employer laid off 75% of my co-workers. I clung to my job for the time-being, but the future of our internet music venture looked bleak. With $100,000 in student loans looming over my head, unemployment scared me to death.

So I was stoked when I scored an interview with the founding duo at a new Beverly Hills talent and branding agency backed by well-funded studios. The CEO was a Hollywood *wunderkind*, and his #2 was a female rocket scientist who happened to be a former fashion-model. Not only did I need this job, I wanted badly to play up to their level.

When the day came, the interview gods were smiling on me, and the conversation went brilliantly. I'm not kidding; it was a thoroughly in-depth yet relaxed discussion of macro-vision and micro-values. We all saw the fields of connected entertainment and content distribution evolving in the same direction. As importantly, my comments were crisp, insightful, and tinged with just the right amount of charming, self-effacing humor.

For over an hour, the two genetic miracles on the other side of the table listened intently, locked with me, eye-to-eye. When our chat ended, we said our goodbyes, and they assured me we would talk again soon.

"Damn right we will," I thought, relief and more than a little confidence oozing from every pore as I waved casually to the receptionist and walked toward the elevator lobby. I felt good. I felt proud. And, when I reached my hand up to scratch my nose, I felt something… some non-trivial *thing* protruding well out of my right nostril.

"No," I said to the empty vestibule. "No. Lord, please, no…NO, NO, NO!!!"

Yes. This foreign body was, without question, an un-missable mass of congealed mucus, dust and pet dander—aka a big, hairy booger.

My heart sank and my lunch rose. This was not good. I pulled on the monster and felt it tug on the back of my skull. The size of a quarter and the shape of a small, earnest bird, it—for who knows how long—had been perched just over my stupid mouth…directly in the sight lines of those I so desperately wished to impress.

I examined the beast. It was a dense, beautifully asymmetrical, USDA-certified-organic booger of heft and gravitas: a state-fair-blue-ribbon, steroid-fueled Boogersaurus. In a time before social media, it deserved its own Instagram account. Was it juicy? Like a summer peach.

Oddly—in that moment of shame—I found myself proud to have sired this Platonic ideal of Boogerness. Had I been on the golf course, I would have shown it to my buddies and boasted, "Hey fellas, look what just came out of my face!"

When it comes to nose dirt, however, context matters. An A+ on the links is an F- in an interview. While my word hole had been delivering pithy insights about the future of digital, this booger was screaming "Paul Ollinger Is A Filthy Animal! Do *not* hire him!" Which is why they had been staring me dead in the eye! Had they dared to gaze down, they would have busted out laughing. All these years later, I still admire the discipline required to maintain their composure until I made it out the door.

Yet, in that moment as I was processing my horror, I realized that they were just a few feet away, rolling on the floor howling, "It kept growing!" and "He thinks he got the job! Ba-ha-haaaa!"

A stronger person would have returned to the office, copped a "my bad," perhaps saving both face and the job. Not me. I tucked my tail and got the hell out of there, swimming hard to escape the sucking vortex of my sinking career.

As you may have guessed, I never heard back from the agency. But I am happy to report that a short time after this interview, Yahoo! plucked our company from the wreckage of the busted internet bubble, giving the remaining employees a paycheck and an excellent new career opportunity.

My point to you today is that you're going to blow a job interview or two. Whether you say the wrong thing, too much of the right thing, or you have your innards hanging out of your face, stuff happens. Try not take it too hard.

But next time, do yourself a favor and prep more thoroughly, check a mirror, shine an iPhone camera up your nose, or do whatever it takes to ensure Shrek isn't rappelling out of your nostrils.

That way you might actually get the job, and you won't have to flick a massive, sticky booger onto the pristine brushed-bronze door of a Beverly Hills elevator.

I hope it's still there.

The Dreaded H-Word

Should labors of love be tax-deductible?
SUBSTACK, FEBRUARY 2024

"A hobby loss refers to any loss incurred while a taxpayer conducts business that the IRS considers a hobby. The IRS defines a hobby as any activity undertaken for pleasure rather than for profit."

—*Investopedia*

"We need to talk about your podcast." Thus read the email from my accountant in reference to my 2022 tax return.

Whether you hear it from your CPA, lawyer, or lover, "We need to talk" means that bad news is coming. This was no exception, as the remainder of his note explained: "I'm concerned that the significant deductions from podcast-related expenses will trigger an IRS audit, due to the Hobby Loss Rule."

Yikes. The threat of an IRS audit is nothing to take lightly. I've been audited before and, while I came out squeaky clean, the process required in-depth forensic homework and consumed weeks of my life. It's not an experience I want to repeat.

But as scary as a lube-free government probe might be, the word in his note that caught my eye and turned my stomach was not The A-word; it was The H-word. He was calling my podcast a "hobby," and—as pathetic as it feels to admit this—it hurt my feelings. Like, a lot.

The IRS Hobby Loss Rules rightfully exist to prevent rich dudes from, for example, buying a ranch and then using its significant, vacation-like expenses to reduce their taxable income. It's a fair policy, but words matter and, according to Wikipedia, "hobby" is a "pejorative term" for someone engaged in a "childish pursuit." To the IRS, one's side—or sole—hustle is legitimate only if it generates revenue. If it does not, then that person is a drooling, navel-gazing dilettante dabbling in a masturbatory vanity project. At least that's how I read it.

Interpreted through the lens of Generally Accepted Accounting Principles, Miles' counsel was dead on—my tens of thousands of dollars in 2022 podcast expenses were way out of proportion to the associated revenue, which equaled…what was the exact sum? Oh yes—zero.

But evaluated through the lens of my fragile ego, my podcast is most definitely not a hobby. Over the past five years, I have recorded hundreds of interviews with people like LL COOL J, Judd Apatow, Ryan Holiday, Andrew Yang, and winners of the Nobel Prize, Heisman Trophy, PGA Championship, and Olympic gold medals. I have more than held my own in conversations with best-selling authors, philosophers, CEOs, university presidents, billionaires, and a member of the House of Lords. Third-party metrics indicate that my audience is in the top .5 percentile of all podcasts worldwide, and people I have never met seek me out to tell me that my work has made them better human beings.

Does that sound like a fucking hobby?

Well, according to the IRS, yes, that's precisely what it is, regardless of how deeply their opinion wounds my pride. Speaking of which, my visceral reaction to their bureaucratic diagnosis warranted reflection as to why I was taking this so personally. I think it's because I've invested so much in my podcast, *Crazy Money*, both financially and emotionally.

Anyone with a smartphone can make a podcast, but the low barriers to entry disguise an ugly truth: producing a decent show is hard and very expensive. On top of recording equipment and software subscriptions, I spend a few hundred bucks per episode for audio editing, which doesn't seem terrible until you multiply it by 40 episodes per year. And there's no upper limit on how much one could spend on guest bookers, publicists, and social media managers, to say nothing of video production, without which you'll miss the growing audiences on YouTube and Spotify and non-optional promotional clips for Insta, TikTok, and Snapchat. But even if you put together a fantastic product and invest loads in marketing, your chances of breaking through the clutter are meager.

On a recent episode of the *Pivot* podcast, Scott Galloway shared with co-host Kara Swisher the harsh financial realities of the 3-million-show podcast universe, saying, "Anything outside of the top 300-500 podcasts are just marketing or hobbies." (Yes, he used that word.) Even with the backing of a massive platform like Spotify, A-List celebrities like the Obamas and the Sussexes couldn't make the investment work, which helps to explain the recent spate of industry layoffs and why the number of net new podcasts is flat or down.

Galloway, who once described indie producers like me as "wannabe Joe Rogans,"[1] went on to tell Swisher that podcasting makes no sense for the creator unless he or she is deriving a lot of "psychic income." My ears perked up. Here was one of those moments of illumination that come when you listen to brilliant people engaged in the kind of long-form, constraint-free conversations you only get on podcasts.

While discussing the potential profit or loss Sirius would incur from its new deal with *Smartless*, Grumpy Prof G dropped some knowledge that struck home. The reason I persevere with *Crazy Money*, despite the massive time commitment and dogshit economics, is because producing my show makes me feel engaged and useful. I learn a lot. I meet incredible people. I provide value for my small but very real audience of curious listeners who often tell me my work matters—that *I* matter. That's why I take it personally.

More to the point, *Crazy Money* is a big part of what I've done with my life over the past half-decade. In addition to being a committed husband, loving father, and pretty good stand-up comic, it's who I am.

---

1   To be clear, Scott didn't mention me, but his statement came just days after I sent him an email invite to be on my show. I don't know if he ever read my note and I'm sure he receives dozens of podcast invitations every week, but how many are from bald comedians who wish they were Joe Rogan?

Lacking a professional title at a recognizable institution, I am "Paul Ollinger, comedian and *podcaster*." Don't you see that, IRS?

When I left my job at Facebook, I tried to articulate to a friend my frustrations with the role-playing that is required in the corporate world, saying, "I'm just trying to find work that feels like me being me." And I've found it. The only downside is that it hasn't paid so great, yet.

I have been asked, "How do you figure out what to do with yourself when you no longer need a paycheck?" Here's my answer. "Ask yourself: what are you willing to spend several years learning to do with no expectation of financial compensation?"

So, if you're going to pursue podcasting or a similar creative endeavor, keep your expectations in check. If there are no barriers to entry for a field that pays significant psychic income, then supply will always exceed demand, profits will be non-existent, and—even if you're in the top .5 percentile of your chosen field—there will be thousands of others between you and the leaders in your category.

These market conditions might prevent me and my fellow podcasters from ever reaching that orgasmic intersection of the *authentic* and the *lucrative*, although I have managed to reduce my burn rate. In 2023, I scraped my way to high-five figures in speaking fees and Substack subscriptions. (Thank you, kind readers!) It's still a money pit, but it's slightly less deep.

The good news is that I love doing the work. And unlike a paycheck, psychic income is not taxable. At least not yet. So don't tell Miles or the IRS that I'm having such a good time.

Managing Sales Quota Stress

There's more to sales than making presentations
LINKEDIN, OCTOBER 2015

Everyone is a seller!" exclaim the self-help gurus promising non-sales professionals higher productivity and fulfillment by leveraging best-in-class sales techniques. "Selling is part of your job, even if it's not part of your job title..." the idea continues, exhorting the positive value of selling to those not otherwise mandated or inclined to do so.

While I understand the sentiment here, I take exception to the notion that "everybody sells." Certainly the vast majority of professionals would be more successful by communicating better and building more positive relationships with their constituents. But being persuasive and asking good questions are not the only aspects of being a seller, and they are certainly not the most challenging.

Anyone who has actually sold for more than a single quota period knows that one is either responsible for a sales goal or one is not. So unless you understand the butt-puckering anxiety of staring at an empty Salesforce pipeline with no freaking idea how you are going to hit that quarter's giant number, then you, my friend, are no Willy Loman.

The hardest thing about sales is the stress of hitting your goal. It is an all-encompassing, world-defining worry wherein the seller's performance is oft-conflated—either tacitly or overtly—with his human value. It starts when you get your number, aka, your target/goal/quota—any one of a number of nouns that are most often preceded by the gerund form of the expletive meaning "to copulate." Your manager calls you into a conference room then presents your astronomical target for the sales period, emphasizing with a straight face that she thinks it is "realistic." How does she do that? She must practice yogic facial-muscle control or something.

If, through a miracle of luck, favoritism, or grift, you have procured a softball number that you are going to rip apart, the only appropriate response is to say, "I'm going to give it my best," and then get the hell out of that room before she changes her mind. The more likely scenario is that you will think, "How in the world am I going to get there?" and your stomach will commence a 90-day churn that will only stop when it's replaced by next quarter's dyspepsia.

But you're a seasoned professional, so instead of screaming, crying, or questioning her sanity, you take a deep breath and query as thoughtfully and professionally as possible: "Can you share some insight as to how management arrived at this number?"

Your esteemed leader will answer with something like, "Well, as you know, Jim, it starts with the overall corporate number, and is divided by business lines and regions. I then allocate my number among the team, using historical trends, forward-looking models, and multi-variable regression analysis."

In a parallel universe you might reply, "In other words, you pulled it out of your ass?" In the same pretend land, she would nod her head cheerily and admit, "Yes. That's exactly right!" But you don't live in pretend land. You live in this office. In this market. In this economy, good or bad. And part of the rights, duties, and privileges pertaining to being a true seller is accepting your number like a team player. So you take it. You swallow it whole. You nod your head and say, "Okay." Then you go home and bury your anxiety under loads of fudge ripple, cheap merlot, and Taylor Swift ballads.

Your massive metric will haunt your sleep, but the next morning you will wake up, look in the mirror, and say to your reflection, "Let's go do it."

You have been here before, so you know how it works. Drawing the short sales-quota straw is like golfing while suffering from severe intestinal discomfort: at a certain point, you've just got to clench your butt cheeks and swing. Then whatever happens happens.

Yet that doesn't stop the self-help authors from opining, "Selling is all about building consensus…."

Sure it is. Tell that to the actual seller who can't open Salesforce without a Xanax and a barf bag.

Mid-Career Burnout Is Real

What to do when your professional career becomes a grind
MEDIUM, APRIL 2021

Bob stared at his iced tea and grilled salmon salad. A senior partner at a regional investment bank, he earns a very substantial income. He had asked me to lunch "just to catch up," but I suspected he harbored a more urgent agenda. And here it was.

"Paul, I still have 15 years left until retirement," he shared solemnly. "I work most weekends, and every morning, I have to drag myself to the office. What am I going to do?"

Since I started my podcast about the connection between money, work, and meaning, I've received many emails from people like Bob: middle-aged and successful on paper, but grappling to maintain a connection to the sterling career that was once the professional cornerstone of a perfect life.

Let's be frank: the melancholy of the affluent corporate types doesn't rank near the top of the world's most pressing problems. But for the employee who is at an age when professional change is difficult, the malaise stemming from exhaustion and a lack of purpose can saturate every corner of their existence. Common work-life balance advice doesn't cut it here. No conversation with a spouse, walk around the block, or fishing trip with their kid—if there's even time for such extravagance—will answer the existential question, "What in hell am I doing with my life?"

I interviewed Yale law professor Daniel Markovits, author of *The Meritocracy Trap*, in which he describes the problem of mid-career burnout. Centuries ago, aristocrats owned assets like coal mines or railroads that generated income while the idle proprietors slept. In contrast, today's elite—well-paid doctors, lawyers, consultants, investment bankers, and the like—earn money only when they show up to do the job. While knowledge is the underlying asset, time is their currency.

Earlier in their careers, people often have more stamina for onerous or even unhealthy demands on their time. But as they age, the zero-sum trade-off between work and personal relationships imposes an increasingly burdensome tax on their soul. Worse yet, the higher they ascend on the ladder, the more of their time is required. As a lawyer friend of mine summarized: "It's a pie-eating contest—and the reward is more pie."

Consider the data: more than half of the top 1% of earning households include one person who works more than 50 hours per week. Men in that same top percentile work 50% longer hours than the men in the bottom half of earners. So while those who really need the income don't get the opportunity to work, elites keep hours that practically eliminate adequate amounts of sleep, exercise, or time with spouses and children.

This is where a lot of the brightest, hardest-working people find themselves and where I encountered my pal Bob and his challenging question. What indeed does a 45-plus-year-old professional do when he finds himself over the barrel of his own success?

The knee-jerk response would be, "Why don't you just quit?" For those who are fortunate enough to have that as a viable financial option, freedom is on the table. But even they can feel trapped. Despite years of juicy bonuses, the expenses of many professionals have grown in lockstep with their rise up the corporate ladder. They treat their generous paychecks like payouts from a slow-motion lottery, locking themselves into lake houses, private schools, and country club memberships that now represent their economic baseline. While this situation might not deserve much empathy, it is an undeniable barrier to a prudent, near-term exit.

Okay, then why not just cut back one's hours and earn a little bit less? This is a great idea in theory, but difficult in practice. Modern professional services firms do not easily accommodate part-time or even "reasonable" workloads. Markovits attributes this failure to a collective practice of using income to "keep score." Whatever the reason, you're never going to hear about a company called Joe's Pretty Good Investment Bank: home of the 40-hour workweek.

After giving it some thought, here are a few things I would recommend to Bob and others who are grappling with this issue:

- **First, honor the gravity of the situation** by hiring a therapist or a professional coach with whom you can explore potential solutions. You should be talking about your problem, but not with me or on social media, or even to your partner if you find yourself complaining ad nauseam.
- **Second, summon patience.** Though your problem feels urgent, a thoughtful change will take time—years, perhaps— to reduce your burn rate, reposition yourself professionally, and find a more hospitable work home. Lawyers can secure in-house positions on the client-side. Financial and consulting types can explore CFO, controller, or strategy positions. Not that these jobs are cakewalks, but they generally come with a more manageable lifestyle and a direct connection to an ongoing concern.
- **Lastly, check your reserves of personal strength.** When you're stressed at work, you need to have your best personal game going. Tap the brakes on the booze. Carve out time to get to the gym and check where you're spending your energy at work. If a political battle presents itself, ask yourself whether the time and focus required to engage it will enrich or deplete you.

Along these lines, be careful not to blow yourself up. Every day may feel like a crisis, but it's not. You're in a good place. Recall that the job you have today is a gig you once dreamed of. You looked up to the person who held your current position, and today there are dozens of younger people who hold you in admiration. (Note: don't sleep with them.)

If you're one of these younger professionals, be aware that now is the time to prepare yourself for the coming mid-career burnout. Manage your lifestyle so that you always have "walk-away money" and keep an eye out for the kind of "niche" jobs that provide a good income and self-determination but don't require you to sell your soul.

Burnout might feel like a long way off, but before you know it, you may find yourself asking a friend for help over iced tea and salmon salad.

White Whale Career Metaphor Acid Dream

I think it was chicken vindaloo

SUBSTACK, JULY 2023

In the trippy world of my dreams, I stepped up to the counter and greeted the cruise director. "Good morning. I'm Paul Ollinger in C-112. I think there's an issue with our itinerary."

"Yes, Mr. Ollinger, what seems to be the trouble?" replied the kind woman in a crisp maritime uniform.

"I recall having signed up for the 'Luxurious Do Nothing on the Beach' package with the chaise lounges, foot massage, and a free rum punch. But this sheet describes today's activity as 'Pursuit of Deadly Career Leviathan.'"

"May I see that, sir?" she said, taking my personalized schedule, then reading aloud, *"...stalk giant, elusive, and incredibly dangerous vocational whale in an authentic 19th-century schooner with a crew of madmen, cannibals, and a bat-shit insane captain. Expect to be wet, cold, and miserable. Side effects include vomiting, scurvy, and gut-wrenching self-doubt."*

"Does that come with the rum punch?" I inquired.

She answered, "No sir, I'm afraid it doesn't. They may offer some musty ale, but you'll have to fight off the harpooners for your share."

"I was kidding," I said, drearily.

"Well, sir. It looks like you originally signed up for the beach day, but at some point changed tack to the whaling trip."

"Miscommunication with the wife," I replied, unwilling to acknowledge my error. "Are there any other activities available? Wave-runners? Dolphin encounter? Cooking class?"

"No, sir. But the good news is that you will have no other passengers on your whaling excursion with you. You get the crew all to yourself."

"Delightful," I said, scanning further down the page. "And what is this about the 'complete waiver of responsibility'?"

"Oh yes sir, we require that you release the cruise line from all responsibility since nine-out-of-ten passengers who take this adventure disappear forever."

"Ninety percent never come back?" I asked. "Why would anyone sign up for that?"

"You tell me, sir," she replied. "This dream is your analogy."

"It's a metaphor!" I demanded, much too defensively.

"As you wish—your *metaphor*. Speaking of which, what do you think it all means?"

"I suppose the cannibals and harpooners represent other comedians with whom I have cast my career lot," I offered. "And the whale theme is…"

"…you want the reader to know that you finally finished *Moby Dick*!" She said, completing my thought.

"The unabridged version!" I added, proudly.

"Good for you," she chimed with a smirk and a golf clap. "Then who am I, besides a convenient conversational artifice?"

"Perhaps you're my conscience? My soul? A dormant childhood fantasy about Vicki Stubing from *The Love Boat*?"

"Hey—not so dormant!" she said with a wink. Then she got serious. "Sir, we'll do our best to accommodate your wishes, but you should think through what you're really committed to, as we charge meaningful fees for changing your itinerary."

"It seems so."

"But it's your cruise, Mr. Ollinger, so just say what you're looking for, and we'll make it happen."

For a moment, I considered my options. "So, the sitting on the beach thing—that's still available?"

"Whenever you say so, sir."

"Do people enjoy that?"

"Frankly, when passengers come back from the beach, they don't look unhappy *per se*. They just look a little sleepy from all the sun and punch."

"But when they return from the whale hunt...." she began.

"*If* they return." I corrected, perhaps too aggressively.

"*If* they return...." she complied. "They look...enthralled."

"Right," I said, shaking my head. "Do I get my money back if we catch zero orcas, humpbacks, or narwhals?"

"I'm afraid we provide no refunds or guarantees, sir. We offer only the pursuit itself. What happens out there, well...." she trailed off.

"So there's a good chance I'll die, a 100% chance I'll be uncomfortable, and I won't get to sit my ass on the beach with a free rum punch?"

"Correct."

"Geez. What an option," I grumbled.

Having heard enough of my whining, she dropped her smile and got in my face. "Hey dumbass, can I ask you something?"

"Sure."

"Do you really like rum punch?"

"Of course not. It's diluted bottom-shelf liquor mixed with syrupy canned juices. You serve your bovine customers a complimentary goblet at breakfast, which gives them the excuse they're looking for to get drunk and do nothing with their day."

"Exactly. It's an opiate and a marketing ploy for suckers," she said. "Is that how you want to spend your time here?"

She let me ponder this for a moment as I considered my options.

"No," I answered sheepishly. "It's just that—well, even if I survive—what if I don't see any whales out there?"

"That's a definite possibility, sir," she replied. Then she smiled, tilted her head, and offered, "But what if you do?"

Guardrails Are Good

How Tony Hsieh's death demonstrates our need to work
MEDIUM, JANUARY 2021

As I've noted elsewhere in these essays, after almost two decades grinding away in the corporate world, I quit my job at 42. I didn't have a plan, but I did have some money and decided I would use it to live a life free from the stress of professional employment. Because not working is the ultimate dream, right?

A few months later, I found myself sitting on the couch, shoving Pirate's Booty into my bored face, and enduring constant heckling from the annoying neighbor between my ears. That brain, lacking work's daily responsibilities and long-term goals, cried out for a purpose: "We should be famous," Brain told me. "Let's make a bomb!"

"Whoa, tap the brakes, Brain!" I said. "I understand that you're bored, but let's start with a podcast and see how it goes."

Eventually, I launched the podcast on which I talk to leading experts about money and purpose. Here's something that keeps coming up in these conversations: no matter how affluent we may become, each of us still needs meaningful work in our lives, lest we fall prey to our weakest impulses and most dangerous appetites.

This fact echoed in my head last month when I read the *Forbes* cover story "Tony Hsieh, American Tragedy: The Self-Destructive Last Months of the Zappos Visionary," which chronicled the former e-commerce executive's descent into addiction and the bizarre behavior that led to his death in a mysterious house fire. While I didn't know Tony, and I'm not a psychologist, I believe that his $700 million+ fortune and a lack of an imperative to work likely catalyzed his demise.

To see the whole picture, one must understand the extent of Tony's extraordinary vision and drive. He joined Zappos as CEO in 1999, the year in which doubts about online shopping's potential pushed Amazon stock down from $105 to $45/share. (It closed recently at $3,165.)

Amidst this early skepticism, Tony created a revolutionary, non-hierarchical culture at Zappos and developed radical customer service practices, like free, no-questions-asked returns that helped eliminate the hesitations of would-be digital consumers. In the process, he grew annual sales to over $1 billion and eventually sold the shoe retailer to the now-dominant Amazon.

Tony also applied his limitless thinking to the broader community. He pushed those around him to dream bigger, invested hundreds of millions of his own dollars to revitalize downtown Las Vegas, and captured his rogue business spirit in a book called *Delivering Happiness*.

Yet despite his passion to help others find happiness, Tony appeared unable to find peace for himself, especially in 2020. According to news accounts, he spent $56 million on real estate in Park City, UT that year to provide full-time lodging for himself and friends, whom he paid up to twice their highest salary ever to come to live with him and "be happy."

While happiness was the stated goal, his compound reportedly took on the feel of a "hedonistic enclave" where pairing psilocybin, DMT, ketamine, and nitrous oxide with sleep deprivation and radical diets drove his weight to below 100 pounds. While partying every day might sound great in theory, at some point, it makes us weaker.

The Book of Proverbs warns that "idle hands are the devil's workshop," but even if you don't believe in the devil, the message is no less accurate: work helps to keep us out of trouble. In his book, *Tribe*, Sebastian Junger argues that vast wealth is an unnatural state of being. Needing nothing from those around us, he says, "falls way outside more than a million years of human experience. Financial independence can lead to isolation, and isolation can put people at a greatly increased risk of depression and suicide."

Junger explains how work is a vital component of a meaningful life, fulfilling our need to feel competent, authentic, and connected to others. But beyond the warm-fuzzies we earn from cool co-workers and a job well done, work provides another component that keeps us from going over the edge: accountability.

"The most significant motivator (to get drug or alcohol) treatment—especially for men—is the boss." That's what Dr. Drew Pinsky, the well-known physician and addiction specialist, told me when I asked him if work's daily guardrails help protect us from ourselves. "If the boss says 'get treatment, or you're going to lose your job,' men go into treatment."

Sadly, Tony didn't have a boss whose warnings might have straightened him out, and a lot of his money seems to have gone toward purchasing the isolation Junger cautioned against. The resulting death is a sad reminder that wealth and contentment, while not mutually exclusive, are also not synonymous.

Having lots of money doesn't change who a person is, but it does allow the possessor to choose where on the spectrum of behavioral potential he will operate. That doesn't mean every rich person is doomed to a spiral of depression, indolence, or drug binges. Nor does having a job necessarily protect us from addiction.

But our idle hands and brains are like unsupervised children—if they don't have constructive activities to channel their natural impulses and energy, they're going to find trouble. If we're lucky, the extent of that mischief will be a pretty good podcast and a couch smeared with Pirate's Booty.

Burn Your Boats!

Cortés had second thoughts. You will too.
MEDIUM, MAY 2021

Quit your job.
That's what the cult of potential-achievement wants from you. They *dare* you to pull the ripcord, probing on their podcasts and Substacks: "What would you do if you weren't afraid?" implying that anyone with a steady paycheck is a corporate cream puff.

Modern ninjas, they preach, live awesomely off-the-grid through entrepreneurship, the arts, or kite-surfing-mountain-climbing-veggie-juice-fasting in Bali. To make the point, these performance provocateurs cite historical badassery such as Spanish conqueror Hérnan Cortés who, upon landing the fleet in Mexico, demonstrated his commitment to the mission by torching his ships. This, you must agree, was the most rad bro-tivational move ever, because in 1519 there was no UberX, let alone an uberFLOTILLA.

Since I abandoned a very lucrative career in digital media to pursue life as a stand-up comedian, I know a little bit about the tenacity of dreams and the realities of boat-burning. My informed point-of-view leaves me convinced that the Cortés headline ("Conquistador Blazes Barges, You Should Too") tells only half the story, and that, in a moment of post-combustion clarity, Cortés summoned his second-in-command (Joe) to inquire on the state of his fleet. Here's how it went down:

CORTÉS: Emm, just curious here, my good chap…. (*Cortés sounded a lot like John Cleese*) Did we, in fact, burn *all* the boats?

JOE: Oh yes we did, sir. You made a most spectacular blaze of those crafts.

CORTÉS: "You don't say. It seems my recollection is a bit foggy from all the adrenaline and sherry…."

JOE: "A dram or ten passed your lips, sir, but you were all the more inspiring for it!"

<Sweat beads on the captain's forehead>

CORTÉS: "So good to hear."

JOE: "Never have I heard a more dramatic rallying cry! You summoned the crew to conquer not just the savages, but the boundaries of their hearts and souls."

CORTÉS: "I said that?"

JOE: "Sir, do you not recall? You exhorted the men to set flame to the boats, then dispatched to both His Highness and His Holiness a lengthy memo with the SUBJ line, "*Adios, pendejos.*""

CORTÉS: "Really?"

JOE: "You CC'ed the entire Armada."

CORTÉS: "Oh dear. What else did the missive contain?"

JOE: "Lots of good stuff about forging your own way, eating what you kill, and assorted quotes from the *Cuatro Horas Work Week*."

CORTÉS: "Powerful stuff."

<the cringing Cortés brings his palm to his cheek and continues>

CORTÉS (cont.): "Tell me, Leftenant, did we spare any vessel at all—perhaps a modest dinghy?"

JOE (chuckling): "Oh no, sir. You insisted on a most comprehensive conflagration."

CORTÉS (lamenting): "If nothing else, I'm thorough."

JOE: "Sir, are you having second thoughts about our mission?"

CORTÉS: "Oh no! No, no, no…. Well…yes."

JOE: "But didn't you say "jump and the parachute will appear"?

CORTÉS: "I read that on a Successories poster. I thought it sounded cool."

JOE: "Oh."

CORTÉS: "And it's not "second thoughts" so much. I'm just getting a touch nostalgic about those old boats of ours. They were grand, weren't they? What with their ample salary, health benefits, and unlimited free snacks."

JOE: "The snacks were nice."

CORTÉS: "I'm not so deluded as to pretend the seas were always calm. Remember Q2, 1507?"

JOE: "How could I forget? For 90 days I was covered in my own sick!"

CORTÉS: "But we made it through together!"

JOE: "We had the nautical charts after all."

CORTÉS: "I do miss maps!"

JOE: "Riiiight? Who knew they were such a luxury?"

CORTÉS: "What I wouldn't give for a good cartographer."

<the two stand together in silence for a moment as the subordinate ponders his boss's words….>

JOE: "Sir, this might not be my place, but…have you considered hiring a career coach?"

<aaand, SCENE>

Luckily for the Spaniards—less so for the Aztecs—Cortés composed himself, then got his plunder on.

Here's the point of this highly contrived parable: elective, mid-career reinvention comes at a very high cost. So before you douse your cubicle with kerosene, you might consider some of the things I've learned:

- **Do it only if ye can't *not* do it.** However challenging you believe it will be to do comedy, make the senior tennis tour, or disrupt the Grilled Cheese Industrial Complex[2] with your networked Panini app (!), it's going to be *way* harder than you think. If you can stomach a traditional career, you might want to stick with it.
- **Check your provisions.** Even if you're already wealthy, making zero money year after year is a huge drag and will make you question your mission a thousand x a thousand times, especially when you see your old colleagues continue to move forward, heaping on the dough and professional accomplishments. Strap yourself to the mast, Odysseus, because dreams are the siren songs that will steer your ship into the poor house, if only on a relative basis.
- **It's not just the booty.** A paycheck is more than cash. It's a third-party validation of your value. When those "you matter" pings disappear from your bi-weekly sonar, you will inevitably start to wonder, "what the hell am I doing with my life?" You'll also learn that your old shipmates —coarse and reeking of grog though they were—provided laughs, support, and, if nothing else, a break from those pesky voices in your head.
- **Know your destination.** You may find someone to put you on stage or fund your idea with a little seed money, but the initial euphoria of "doing your thing" will dissipate quickly and be replaced by "How do I do my thing at scale?" which will

---

2   When reviewing years of essays all-in-a-row, I see words, phrases and concepts that I repeated. If you've read this book from start to this point, you recognize "networked pannini app." I am choosing to leave it in.

likely take years to figure out. If you can't answer this question, keep your career away from open flame.
- **Check your mate's resolve.** If you're single and plan to remain so forever, then do whatever you like. But if you're committed to another person or a family, you need them on board. After all, your work has a meaningful impact on household harmony. Sooner or later you're going to hear, "If you're not having any fun, why don't you just go back to your old job? Heck, they had free snacks!"

I'm not saying don't do it. Just make sure you're doing it based on what's in your heart and not because some dude on Instagram thinks he knows what's right for you.

Whatever you decide, *buen viaje* and *buena suerte!*

An Inadequate Tribute to Dave Goldberg

Reflections on a good friend's life
LINKEDIN, MAY 2015

When you start a new job, you never really know what's in store. Maybe the job won't be that great and you'll stick around for only a few months. Perhaps things will go pretty well and the job will provide income, benefits, and a decent working environment for several years.

Or maybe, unbeknownst to you, you'll have hit the jackpot and landed in a vortex of brilliant, passionate people, working in a burgeoning industry at a great, young company led by a CEO who will become not just your friend, but a mentor and advocate, for the next 18 years.

I didn't know it then, but that is exactly what happened to me in 1997 when I joined LAUNCH Media, the digital music company co-founded by Dave Goldberg, the friend, dad, husband, brother, son, and Survey Monkey CEO who passed away on Friday ~~2015~~.

With LAUNCH, Dave and co-founder Bob Roback, a whip-smart attorney who scared me then as much as he cracks me up now, broke new ground in digital music and built a great culture that reflected their personal values. Both guys were brilliant but modest. They hired hard-working dreamers who shared their love of music and technology, creating a virtuous garden for careers and decades-long friendships.

From the ranks of LAUNCH, which later became Yahoo! Music, rose dozens of outstanding leaders in the digital media industry. The CEOs of Beats Music, Vimeo, and Kin Community, the President of

Disney Interactive (now Chairman of ESPN) and many, many more senior folks earned stripes at our young start-up.

I think there's both cause and effect at work here. The best and brightest wanted to work for Dave because he was not only crazy smart but also a genuinely good guy. Then, having learned from his wisdom and example, they were ready for bigger and better opportunities when the time came.

Dave set the tone of humility and transparency. He was never haughty when we were flying high on the helium of the dotcom bubble. Nor was he gloomy when the bubble burst, though I know it hit him hard.

Dave took care of his people. He brought us into his world and spread the fun of working in the music industry around. In my first month on the job, I got to see Radiohead's afternoon sound-check at the 9:30 Club in Washington D.C. where we were filming for its inclusion in the LAUNCH CD-ROM. That night, though he barely knew me, Dave invited me to share dinner with him and his friend who worked at the Treasury Department. Her name was Sheryl Sandberg.

Later that year, Dave took me to the New York premiere of *Good Will Hunting,* which was produced by his friend Chris Moore and partially edited in the LAUNCH offices. When our editorial team interviewed rock gods Jimmy Page and Robert Plant, Dave ensured that I got to meet them too, with the gentle guidance, "Just be cool, okay?" (I don't think I was...but Dave never called me on it.)

Perhaps my most special memory of Dave was a night in 2003. I had moved to Northern California to join the Yahoo! national sales team and was side-lining in a fledgling stand-up comedy career. Dave was up from LA for meetings and insisted on joining me at a post-work open mic a few miles from the Yahoo! campus.

Here's this guy running a big chunk of Yahoo!'s business, but he's still got time to come hear me tell fart jokes at a bar in Cupertino. Yet he wasn't just present—he was the guy laughing the loudest. Exactly as he was the last time I saw him, at the Consumer Electronics Show (CES) in January when he permitted me to practice my rusty stand-up at his and (his hilarious brother/my close friend) Rob's dinner for some of the top folks in media and technology. Dave's signature laugh reached peak volume when the jokes were about him.

That was Dave. He was every bit as excited about your dreams as he was about his own. He would leverage his considerable brain and network to help you achieve them however he could. It is that investment in other people that you see manifest in the massive outpouring of love since his death. Because Dave didn't just do these nice things for me or for a handful of special people—he did them for *everybody*.

One time in the years after I left Yahoo!, I flew to Las Vegas for a comedy festival. I hadn't seen Dave or Rob for a while, but we had shared many a good time in Vegas in the years prior. Waiting in the cab stand at McCarran Airport, I texted them with a message something to the extent of: "Just landed in Vegas. Can't help but think about you jokers whenever I'm here."

Within minutes, Dave texted back: "I'm at the Bellagio. Come over."

Of course he was there. Dave was always there. Not "in Vegas" there, but "there" there. He was always there to help. He was there to listen. To offer advice. To make a helpful suggestion and/or an introduction. To encourage you or to gently re-direct your thinking. He was there like the amazing big brother he was to Rob and as the friend and mentor he was to the rest of us. He was our accessible, anchored source of wisdom who knew everyone and, seemingly, everything.

In the past 48 hours, I have been flooded with sadness but also with profound gratitude for the opportunity to have known Dave and benefitted from his vision, knowledge, and friendship. I'm going to miss him a bunch and I'm going to try to follow his example. Because Dave wasn't just the smartest guy in the room. He was also the kindest

LIFE

Every Day Is Thanksgiving

Why we should savor the everyday
SUBSTACK, NOVEMBER 2023

I'm sitting in my car, looking over 25 acres of soccer fields where my son is practicing a sport he loves. I have the windows down, inviting in a little breeze and the sounds of kids and early teens running after a checkered ball. After practice, we'll go home, eat some dinner, put the garbage cans on the street, watch a little TV, then go to bed.

In other words, it's an ordinary day—not a particularly good or bad day. Actually, I'm a little annoyed with a creative project I can't get off the ground and the guys painting our house were supposed to finish today but didn't, which means I'm going to have to park on the street and that's a pain.

Yet, today is an extraordinary day because no one I love is dying. My family is healthy. We have plenty to eat. Tonight, as we sleep in a warm, dry house on clean, white sheets, it's virtually certain that savages won't invade our home and murder us. Nor will bombs rain down on us from the skies. This is worth remembering.

Let's be honest, there's not a whole lot you can do to stop the deaths of innocent people in Israel and Gaza. The parties there have been at war for 75 years—or 2,000, depending on when you start counting—and the most powerful diplomats in the world have failed to come up with a solution. If Jimmy Carter and Bill Clinton, with the full weight of the United States government behind them, can't make meaningful progress, then your thoughts, prayers, and protests aren't going to move the needle either.

Maybe the best thing we can do for the world, but definitely for ourselves, is to make the conscious choice to be grateful that we don't live in a war zone. So while trivial annoyances clamor for my attention, I am taking this moment right here and now to remind myself: if things aren't bad, they're good. Very good.

If you're reading this, it's because your government permits the free exchange of ideas. You have a computer or a smartphone, running on a functioning electrical grid, and an equally functional brain that provides you with both the ability to reason and *exceptionally* good taste in writers. At least logistically, you're in a good place.

Of course, myriad frustrations present themselves to us every day. Some a-hole cuts you off in traffic, something happens at the kids' school that offends your political sensibilities, and no matter how you try, you cannot figure out how to work your new air fryer. Who would build such a nonsensical user interface?!

But never forget that real pain is all around you. Right up the street from the soccer fields is a Ronald McDonald House where parents of terminally ill children are barely holding it together. Somewhere on the sidelines is a person who just lost a parent or sibling. And the currently stable political fabric that prevents us from killing each other should never be taken for granted.

All over Atlanta, historical markers call out significant events in the city's history, the majority about events leading up to the Battle of Atlanta during the Civil War. There are so many of these signs—literally hundreds—that you stop noticing them.

I'm trying to notice—to stop and read, for example, about a group of young men not much older than my son who camped at Nancy Creek, which runs adjacent to these very soccer fields, a few days before marching south to a battlefield where thousands of them died in a single day 159 years ago.

When you find yourself stressed out by the haters and the users, catatonically bored by life's minutiae, or caught in a vicious cycle of rumination and self-talk, try to zoom out. Some of you might be dealing with some very serious stuff in your life right now and, if so, I wish you strength. But if you're not fighting off cancer or creditors, if you're not dealing with death or divorce, if your house isn't on fire and missiles aren't heading toward your face, take five minutes to remember that your problems are quite manageable or—more likely—not problems at all.

Life so often feels like we've got sand in our underwear—as if, despite all we have, something isn't quite right. Like, somewhere out there is a lost email account with all the opportunities that never found us, and things would be okay *if we could just find that inbox.* This idea is entirely self-created and the way to break out of it is to choose to acknowledge that you are above ground and lucky as fuck.

David Letterman asked Warren Zevon what the singer's soon-to-be fatal mesothelioma had taught him about life: "From your perspective now," Dave asked, "do you know something about life and death that maybe I don't know?"

Zevon took a breath and responded, "Not unless I know how much you're supposed to enjoy every sandwich."

How brilliant. No one sandwich seems terribly significant until you recognize that—if you're incredibly fortunate, as most of us are—life is just a series of sandwiches and naps and showers and shits and Zoom meetings and soccer practices. Whether these events are glorious or soul-crushing tedium depends entirely on our perspective.

So take the time to toast the bread on today's turkey on wheat. Spread on a little extra mayo, and, hell, grab some lettuce and a fresh tomato from the fridge and slice it just the way you like it. When you take that first bite, savor the combination of textures and the small symphony of meat, salt, and fat hitting your taste buds all at the same time, and chew just a little longer than normal because this sandwich isn't just a sandwich, it is a goddamn feast and proof that, at least for now, you are here.

Today's a great day to be on the field of life. Get out there and play.

This Is Us

Inconclusive thoughts on why we kill each other
SUBSTACK, OCTOBER 2023

> "(Dylann Roof) stated clearly that his situation is like a Palestinian in an Israeli jail after killing nine people. He said the Palestinian would not be upset or have any regret because he would have successfully done what he tried to do."
>
> —*Psychiatrist's report on Dylann Roof*

A few years back, a woman I knew in college murdered her husband. She and I weren't close, but we had many friends in common and sometimes I ate at the same table with her in the walnut-paneled refectory of our very respectable private liberal arts institution.

I remember learning the details of the crime: she didn't just kill her husband, she strangled him—an act that requires much greater resolve than simply pulling a trigger. I thought to myself, "Wow, I know a murderer," which was weird because the killers I'd seen in the news always looked like people I would never meet. But here was a person with whom I had actually shared lunch. What would make someone like her—by extension, like me—end a life, and gruesomely so?

I've been thinking about this question for the past ten days. Watching the news about the atrocities in Israel, I've heard the Hamas terrorists referred to as "animals," "monsters," and "inhuman," and I have found myself nodding along in agreement, unconsciously reassuring myself that they are another species altogether. But here's the thing: they too are human—very human. They are us at our absolute worst.

We live on an ethical spectrum. At one end is the gentle person who loves not just his family but his neighbor, even his enemy. Somewhere down the line is a stylish, bi-polar wife with a tourniquet, followed by Dylann Roof in a Charleston church. Despite their different circumstances and motivations, each is human. It makes you wonder just what determines our place on that continuum.

Stacey and I recently watched a documentary called *Ordinary Men: Reserve Police Battalion 101 and the Final Solution in Poland,* based on a book by the same name by Christopher Browning. It tells the story of a squad of middle-aged German men who were too old for the infantry. Instead, these regular, working-class guys were assigned to a "police" squad that rounded up and killed tens of thousands of Jews, including women, children, and the elderly.

These were not political people. They were mechanics, bakers, and the like. Most didn't seem to derive any joy out of their ghastly job and apparently numbed themselves with alcohol and other substances. But when their commander gave the 500-man unit a greenlight to step down, fewer than a dozen did so.

Why? Apparently, their motivations—or at least compliance—were based on "the group dynamics of conformity, deference to authority…and the altering of moral norms to justify their actions." So in addition to mental illness, rage, murderous racism, religious fanaticism, and desperation as catalysts to murder, we have peer pressure. That's right, the alliterative force that drives teenagers to pick up a Parliament or a Pabst also drives grown men to slaughter their fellow persons. What delightful mammals we are!

Understanding the motivations behind heinous acts does nothing to justify them, but there's much to be learned by looking for explanations. While it's tempting to write off Dylann Roof as "evil" or "insane" in the same way we call Hamas non-human, it's chilling to learn of the things they have in common.

After Roof murdered nine black parishioners at Mother Emanuel, a psychiatrist interviewed him to evaluate his mental fitness to stand trial. According to the doctor's report, Roof compared himself to a jihadist and "stated clearly that his situation is like a Palestinian in an Israeli jail after killing nine people. He (Roof) said the Palestinian would not be upset or have any regret because he would have successfully done what he tried to do."

Eventually, Roof fired the lawyers who wanted him to enter an insanity plea because the killer feared being labeled mentally ill more than a death sentence. He wrote in his journal, "I want to state that I am morally opposed to psychology," which he went on to describe as "a Jewish invention."

Feel free to re-read those last two paragraphs because they are both non-obvious and true. As a white supremacist, Roof no doubt considers himself superior to Palestinian Arabs. Ironically, he would find plenty of fellow travelers in Hamas.

Humans have been committing murder since Cain killed Abel and it's unlikely we'll ever stop. If we can come to understand the root causes, perhaps we'll do it less. But I'm not holding my breath.

Why the Jews?

The holy roots of anti-Semitism might surprise you
SUBSTACK, NOVEMBER 2023

The Jews killed Jesus.
    Well, didn't they?
    After all, that's what it says in the Bible, right? Let me check. Yep, there it is in Matthew 27, Mark 15, Luke 23, and John 19: Roman governor Pontius Pilate washes his hands and turns Jesus over to the Jews who were chanting "Crucify him, crucify him!"
    I remember reciting these words in church as a child, like untold millions of other Catholic children. Because for almost 2,000 years, these gospels have been passed down from generation to generation as the inerrant Word of the Lord. And while it's hard to discern where tribalism ends and religion begins, the notion that scripture is without error and that Church doctrine is infallible has led to incalculable tragedy for the Jewish people. I wish I would have known this sooner.
    Last weekend I watched a four-hour presentation called *Why the Jews?: The Long and Tragic History of Antisemitism* by Brendan Murphy, who teaches a seminar on the Holocaust at the Marist School, a Catholic high school here in Atlanta. To explain the rift between Jews and Christians, Murphy takes us back to the founding of Christianity. The early Church was made up of Jews who had accepted Jesus as the long-awaited messiah, as opposed to another sect who weren't so convinced. This latter group, known as the Pharisees, evolved into the Jews we know today. Over the first few decades of the nascent faith, the divide between these factions became hostile.

The Jews for Jesus, as Murphy calls them, wrote the Gospels. Murphy's argument, now endorsed by the Archbishop of Atlanta, is that these authors—while telling the story of Jesus' conception, nativity, and ministry—took the opportunity to lay the blame for His crucifixion on their political opponents, the Pharisees. (It was, in fact, the Romans who executed Jesus, along with thousands of other rebellious Jews.)

This allegation was not accidental—it was a smear campaign. Jesus either was or was not the Messiah, so if the Pharisees were right, then the early Christians were wrong. Thus, "In an attempt to legitimize their own view," Murphy says of their writing, "they seek to de-legitimize those who believe otherwise. In fact, they seek to demonize them."

Of course, no one back then could have known the massive impact the Gospels and the Church would have in shaping Western society. And over time, this force continued to define itself by what it wasn't: the hypocritical sect of Jewish vipers and serpents (Matthew 23:33) who supposedly goaded Pilate to let Jesus' "blood be upon us and on our children" (Matthew 27:25).

Boy was it ever!

To the Catholic Church's credit, it reversed this policy in 1965 with *Nostra Aetate*, a declaration exonerating the Jews for the crime of deicide. But the teaching is not well known, the "troublesome" sections of the Gospels weren't re-written, and, even if they were, how can you undo the damage done by 19 centuries of putrid lies? Answer: you can't.

Furthermore, if the Church officially changed its policy four years before I was born, how come:

1. I didn't learn any of this in my twelve years of Catholic school? And,
2. Why did I, as the modern proxy of the Pharisees—again, the Jewish people—chant "CRUCIFY HIM!" CRUCIFY HIM!" during the Stations of the Cross with my uninformed class-

mates at St. Jude the Apostle Elementary in the 1970s and '80s? (hello, fellow Jaguars, I miss you.)

At this point, Protestants and evangelicals might be thinking, "Well, all this information makes me glad I'm not Catholic." Not so fast, ye lovers of Chick-fil-A—wait until you hear about Martin Luther. You see, despite the reformer's courage to stand up to the Roman Church's laughably deceitful practice of selling Indulgences—literal tickets to "Heaven"—Luther was also horrifyingly anti-Semitic.

Consider what he says in his 65,000-word publication, *On Jews and Their Lies*, which sounds like the name of a Proud Boys Subreddit. Luther calls Jews "a base, whoring people" and "poisonous, envenomed worms." But he's just getting started.

He goes on to argue that synagogues should be burned, that Jews' houses should be razed, and that their money should be seized for "safekeeping" unless they converted. A few hundred years later, Luther's Arian brothers would take him at his word while wearing belt buckles boasting, "Gott Mit Uns," or "God With Us."

It boggles the mind.

Did you know all of this? I didn't, which is surprising, given the Church's long tradition of discrediting its opponents. In fairness to Luther, it's worth mentioning that he was, in this way, not unlike other Christian Europeans of his time. But exactly how did the ideology of the sub-human Jew get baked so deeply into the culture?

The author Michael Pollan wrote that "a reigning ideology is a little like the weather: all-pervasive and virtually inescapable." The cultural critic Lionel Trilling reminded us that ideology is not acquired by thought "but by breathing the haunted air."

With their incriminating scripture and the domination of civic life, the inescapable Church polluted the air with anti-Semitism. Church buildings and cathedrals, including Notre Dame in Paris, were—and still are—bedecked with horrific imagery of Jews, sometimes with horns or money bags, sometimes eating pig feces, or sometimes with snakes wrapped around their eyes.

If you wonder where "dirty Jew" or "greedy Jew" come from, here's your answer.

To the peasants of Europe, the stories told in the Gospels and in Church iconography were unassailable truths from indisputable, holy authority. This propaganda morphed into accusations of appalling ritual slaughter—Jews kidnapping Christian children and drinking their blood. If you don't believe me, go to Trent in Italy where you will find a Renaissance building featuring a frieze of a local Christian boy being flayed and consumed by the descendants of the Pharisees. It bears pointing out that this building stands on the location of the former synagogue that was destroyed after the Jews were driven from the town.

In "This Is Us," I wrote of the "moral norms" that led to average Germans rounding up and murdering thousands of Jews. This didn't start with Hitler. It started with a Church that dehumanized the future Holocaust victims as shit-eating, blood-drinking animals because they didn't accept what the Church was selling.

We think we've moved beyond it, but Scripture-based anti-Semitism still haunts the air. *The Passion of the Christ,* directed and co-written by devout Catholic and pronouncedly anti-Semitic Mel Gibson, depicted a bloodthirsty Jewish mob killing Christ. The film, which received tremendous support among the evangelical community, was shown at Joel Osteen's church, was screened for 4,000 pastors, and went on to gross more than $600 million at the box office in 2004 (about $1 billion in 2023 dollars). It's impossible to say how many children saw this church-sanctioned movie, but suffice to assume that it was millions.

"Hang on, Paul—I liked that movie, but I'm not some Nazi or a jihadist who burns babies alive." I get that. But let's remember that Islam has no monopoly on killing in the name of God. It's been a while since Christian atrocities have made the news, but the historical list is longer than the Pope's robe: the mass murder of the Crusades, the torture of the Inquisition, it goes on and on.

Ever heard of the Massacre of Verden? Good Christian emperor Charlemagne beheaded 4,500 Saxons because they wouldn't accept

Jesus as their Lord and Savior. It's the same philosophy as practiced by the early Christians, Martin Luther, and today's jihadists: you don't accept the "one, true faith," so your life has no value. Convert or die, Saxon infidels!

I strongly recommend making time to watch Murphy's presentation, or at least doing some reading on the roots of anti-Semitism. Because the horror we see in the news now is just the latest manifestation of an age-old tradition called "we-know-God-and-you-don't." Be aware of prevailing moral norms and be careful in your convictions, especially if you regard them as inerrant. They might sound benign, but religious certainty can be deadly.

There's a sweet pre-meal blessing I learned as a child. It starts out:

God is great
God is good
Let us thank him for our food

If you were to recite this prayer in the language of Hamas, the first line would read: "Allahu Akbar." Ring a bell?

So translate your prayers into Arabic. If you still feel comfortable reciting them out loud on an airplane, keep teaching them to your children.

What My Dad's Death Taught Me About Life

Lessons from my father on gratitude, service,
and the power of showing up
MEDIUM, NOVEMBER 2020

My dad died the other day. He left this world while napping in his favorite recliner surrounded by his children. He was 93.

Despite my love for and commitment to my father, I have shed zero tears over his passing. I promise I'm not an unfeeling monster (I cried at least once when I took my daughter to see *Wicked*). It's just that, rather than sadness, I have found myself overcome with a profound sense of gratitude for his presence in my life and for everything he taught me.

Nobody chooses their parents or decides how long their parents will live. These are functions of randomness over which we have no control. Though I did nothing to deserve or affect it, by being "assigned" to Bea and Billy Ollinger, I won the parental lottery.

I was born to two parents who loved their children and dedicated their lives to educating and preparing them for life as adults. My folks were smart, kind, and decent human beings who put their kids before their professional ambitions. They prioritized Catholic school over material possessions (and air conditioning). They stayed together for 55 years—because that's just what you do—and they created a loving home where, despite the occasional chaos, I knew I was safe and part of a tribe. In this way, I experienced the greatest privilege I or anyone can receive or give: the gift of dedicated parenting.

Thanks to the good medical care he received, I benefited from my dad's presence until I was 51. He danced at my wedding then got to know and love the two children who arrived a few years later. But Dad's longevity was never a sure thing. He survived two wars, two heart attacks, prostate cancer, decades of congestive heart failure, and, when I was nine years old, a brain injury that could have killed him. I can't begin to get my head around the advantages—logistical, financial, emotional—I reaped because of this good luck.

I think he was aware of his good fortune and radiated that gratitude in his own dignified, cheerful way. He was brilliant, funny, and devout to Christian values and his sense of self. He knew who he was and never tried too hard to impress anyone. He was a great conversationalist because it was never about him. At a party, he would find that guest standing by themselves, then engage him or her in "them-centric" discussion into which he would throw corny jokes and self-deprecating humor.

He died with his head held high. In the last few weeks of his life, his physical and cognitive decline were palpable. I'd ask him, "Dad, how are you doing?" He would reply invariably, "I can't complain."

This was true: it just was not in his DNA to worry about things outside his control. And why should he? He had run his race, and he had done his very best, having lived life on his terms. He had worked his butt off to raise six kids he loved and who loved him back. He walked the walk of his values: faith, humility, and frugality. When I asked him how one prepares for having such a large family, he said, "You just trust in the Lord."

Speaking of my siblings, I've learned a lot through the 10-year process of tending to elderly parents with them. It's an opportunity to serve those who have served you, but it's a hell of a lot of work, and none of it is glamorous. My five brothers and sisters and I have done all we could within the broader circumstances of our careers and families to embrace this duty.

I'd say it's a thankless job, but it's not. When you repay your parents with the love and care they showered on you, you earn the satisfaction of knowing you did your part. So not only did Dad have no regrets, neither do I. I didn't just tell him I loved him regularly through those final years; I showed him I loved him by showing up to help. Guess who taught me to do that.

When you live for others while being true to yourself, regrets will find no purchase in your heart. And if you live your love for your parents, you will have nothing to regret the day they doze off in their favorite chair.

Lessons from a Freshman Pimple

What acne can teach us about adulthood

SUBSTACK, JANUARY 2023

If I look closely in the mirror, I can see a faint scar from a pimple that plagued my nose for most of October 1983.

One morning, early in my freshman year, my reflection greeted me with a bulging, red honker sticking off the end of my beak, blinking at the world like Rudolph's schnoz. My heart sank. I was 45 days into high school, had not yet found my social footing, and was desperate for people to like me.

I wanted, more than anything, for that pimple to go away. But it was round, hard, and unripe, so its demise was nowhere in sight, unlike the growth itself. This was a problem.

Every grown-up knows that you can't rush a pimple. Sure, you can keep the area clean and apply a warm compress and some Clearasil. Regardless, you still have to wait it out—give it a few days until it comes to a head, then destroy it with a pinch and a splat.

But I didn't know this in the month that "The Safety Dance" was the #1 song on the radio. My mother, who had seen loads of blemishes on my other siblings (and presumably herself), advised me to ignore it. But she was old—like 45 or something—so what did she know about the social pressures of ninth grade?

No, this disaster demanded action! So, I poked. I prodded. I squeezed that bulbous bastard until my eyes watered, but it just wouldn't break. Finally, out of utter desperation, I brandished nail scissors to cut off the pimple's top layer of skin.

In almost all cases, amateur surgery is a bad idea. This case was no exception. My sloppy incision turned an otherwise run-of-the-mill zit into a bloody, festering wound. Instead of going away within the week, it stuck around for the rest of the month. All because I just couldn't leave it alone.

With every passing day, my embarrassment drove me to more desperate measures. One dreary Monday morning, my attractive homeroom tablemate, Mary Kay, asked me, "Paul, at the football game on Friday, were you wearing concealer on your nose?"

"What? No," I lied to her beautiful face, every syllable another log on the fire of my shame. "Why would I do that?"

Of course I'd worn concealer. I had slathered on my sister's Oxy 10 Cover in a futile attempt to distract the world from my tragic flaw, then lied about doing so. Puberty was not off to a good start.

First, do no harm.

In time, my face healed. But the experience taught me a lot. The obvious lesson is that many problems, perhaps most, are best resolved by leaving them alone or applying very limited remedies. As I am still learning: adult life requires determining which disagreements with a colleague, friend, or spouse require taking a stand and which do not.

Hippocrates advised, "First, do no harm." This implies that you should not mutilate yourself with nail scissors, but also that, when confronting problems with others, you should choose the words or actions that do the least amount of damage. If your boyfriend or girlfriend says something insensitive, your cousin posts something ugly on social media, or some crazy lady flips you off on the highway, the best reaction is no reaction. It will save you time, stress, and the road rage of someone who might be packing a Glock in her handbag.

One of the best ways to let things go is to worry less about what other people think. If I could go back and plant one certainty into my teenage brain, it's this: nobody else really cares about your pimple. They only care about *their* pimples or other perceived imperfections, like their height, body type, or the shape of their goofy ears.

As we get older, the things that stoke our insecurity change. Instead of stressing over acne, we worry about our status, money, and relative social position. In an attempt to cover up this anxiety, we injure ourselves by over-spending on junk we don't need. We sacrifice economic autonomy on the altar of perception.

And guess what? In the same way your peers didn't really care about your pimples, they don't now care about your new car, fancy vacation, Hermes belt, or lack thereof. They either have their own stuff, covet yours, or just don't give a toss because they've learned none of those things truly matter.

Mary Kay didn't really care about my pimple, and I made it worse by trying to pretend I was perfect. But I eventually learned to let it go and reaped the rewards—at a party a few years later, she let me touch her boobs.

Why Talking About Money and Happiness Matters

What we can learn from Bono, Brian Cox, and Jonah Hill
SUBSTACK, FEBRUARY 2023

For four years, I've been exploring the connection between money and happiness on my podcast, Crazy Money. I come at the topic mostly through conversations with highly accomplished people and authors who study fulfillment.

Sometimes I wonder if the mission is worthwhile. Or did I just reverse-engineer an idea that fits my experience of having made some money and wrestled with its often-confusing impact on my life. Either way, I found it interesting when the universe—or maybe it was just my Facebook news feed—recently presented copious evidence that the struggle for money and status is an unavoidable human tendency that begs our understanding.

Over the Christmas holiday, I inadvertently came across the work of three well-known artists who offer insights into their own struggles with money. In U2 lead singer Bono's memoir, *Surrender*, Jonah Hill's Netflix documentary, *Stutz*, and the Channel 5 (UK) series, *How the Other Half Live with Brian Cox*, each of these masters of craft confesses to the difficulty they've had handling success or, more specifically, how their struggle to handle life's challenges drove them to succeed.

It speaks volumes that on the second page of a 557-page book, covering over four decades of U2's epic creative accomplishment, Bono writes:

> There are some dirty little secrets about success that I'm just waking up to. And from. Success as an outworking of dysfunction, an excuse for obsessive-compulsive tendencies. Success as a reward for really, really hard work, which may be obscuring some kind of neurosis.

It's not the only thing, and perhaps not the most important, but one of the primary conclusions this international superstar and humanitarian wants you to know: maybe all the accolades and fame are as much the result of the quiet despair he's harbored since losing his mother at age 14 as they are the by-product of his innate work ethic. The suddenly motherless Bono couldn't win the attention of his emotionally paralyzed, widower father, so he set out to win the world's adulation instead.

Is it over-simplification? Maybe. But it makes sense.

Similarly, in *Stutz*, Jonah Hill introduces us to his therapist, Phil Stutz, who has helped the actor, writer, and two-time Oscar nominee grapple with childhood inadequacy that even a dazzling Hollywood career can't extinguish. Jonah sought Phil's help at a time when he had "an incredible amount of success," but also an intense "desperation to get happier." Despite his fame and serious Hollywood cred, Jonah still saw himself as a "14-year-old kid with acne who is very overweight… and feels very undesirable to the world."

Before Jonah found Phil's unique set of coping tools, he engaged in an If/Then relationship with his career. "I thought, if I got successful, they wouldn't see (the fat kid)."

Jonah doesn't specify who "they" are, but he elaborates on his thinking that "success and awards will absolve me of the pain of life," and "…when it didn't cure any of that stuff, it made me beyond depressed."

Yes, Jonah Hill still worries about who he was in middle school. So do I (remember that pimple essay a few chapters back?), and—I suspect, on some level—so do you. As Stutz told *Esquire* in an interview about the problems of movie stars: "at the end of the day, after you get done flying privately or being recognized, the problems are the same. Exactly the fucking same."

Third, Brian Cox, the Scottish actor who grew up destitute but now makes millions portraying media magnate Logan Roy on HBO's *Succession*, just released a mini-series for which his goal is, "to find out what money does to you, to me—how it affects all our lives" because "money is very much my own personal demon—something I've avoided confronting until now."

All this talk by the most prosperous and prolific creators about the nature of success begs the question: *Why?* Why are these wildly accomplished dudes bringing their struggles with accomplishment to the surface, for everyone to see? They need neither the work nor our pity, and I doubt any editor, producer, or publicist begged them to talk about how hard it is to be rich and famous.

I think these guys want to share a secret that only a small number of people who make it to the financial mountaintop learn: wealth doesn't deliver the existential glee almost all of us believe it will. These stars want others to understand that our faith in the redemptive power of money and fame is wildly misplaced.

Before I made some money, I thought wealth would get me more than a big house and some cool cars. I actually believed, if only on a subconscious level, that it would liberate me from the slow-burn anxiety I feel every day. That its attainment would scrub away my self-doubt and the persistent, nagging feeling that I don't deserve to be happy.

Looking back, it's easy to see how silly this is. I spent years working my ass off, thinking, "I'll show those motherfuckers!" I never stopped to specify who "those motherfuckers" were, but when the intense labor led to big bucks, I didn't feel any different. I started wondering, "Wait, which motherfuckers was I going to show?"

We think achievement will vanquish our straw man opponents who have been conspiring to keep us down, but we learn quickly that—while money can buy all kinds of cool stuff and experiences—it can't buy freedom from the voices in our heads. Like Bono's dad and Jonah's non-specific "they," our negative self-talk is the real "those motherfuckers," who we've been trying to outrun the whole time!

So maybe my quest to explore money, happiness, and their relationship isn't a contrived and self-indulgent exercise after all. Maybe if we are more self-aware of how we define success, and what it can and can't do for us, we could pursue the things that really do pay off. More importantly, we could focus on the core issues that hold us back from loving ourselves.

Yeah, or maybe my doubts about the sincerity of my mission is just one more of those motherfucking voices in my head.

.

A Stoic Thought Exercise: What if it All Goes Away?

Meditating on our death might sound like a downer, but it can help us be more grateful

MEDIUM JANUARY 2021

A couple weeks ago, I felt a dull ache in my abdomen. It wasn't painful, but it was persistent and, since the belly houses several mission-critical organs, I decided to get it checked out. My doctor seemed puzzled by my nonspecific symptoms, especially since a recent colonoscopy and upper GI scan indicated all was good. Out of an abundance of caution, he ordered a slew of tests and an ultrasound, which he scheduled for the next afternoon.

After I left my samples and departed the office, I spent the next 24 hours googling "stomach pain" while contemplating my imminent death. The internet suggested I had either a kidney infection, early-stage liver disease, or The Big C. *How would I tell my wife? Who would raise my kids?* I wondered as I cursed the decades of cheeseburgers, french fries, and microbrews that had led me to this inauspicious end.

After torturing myself for almost a full day, I let out a grateful breath when I learned the ultrasound saw only healthy tissue, and my myriad specimens signaled that all organs were working as they should. So, what was the cause of my intestinal discomfort? Gas. That's right, after all that, my only ailment was a lonely, vagrant fart. I didn't require surgery or chemo, just a little Gas-X.

One of life's great tragedies is the degree to which most of us take "normal" for granted. Prior to my little gassy scare, I rarely considered how good it is to "not be sick." It's only when mortality grabs us by the collar, jabs its finger in our face, and screams, "Hey asshole—this 'life' shit is temporary!" that we are stirred from our daily routine of navel-gazing, catastrophizing, and obsessing over minutiae. For a short time, we forget the trivial nonsense, hug our loved ones more tightly, and think, "I am alive."

Luckily, you don't need a personal crisis to experience this feeling of deep gratitude. In a recent episode of my podcast, I spoke to William Irvine, a professor of philosophy at Wright State University, about the practice of negative visualization, which the Stoics used to reflect on the ephemeral nature of our world. The exercise can help all of us see the bigger picture and enjoy—even celebrate—the times when things are just…normal. "You learn how to appreciate things that are already there," Irvine told me. "So you don't need to go off chasing new and different things."

Try it: for just a minute, close your eyes and think of specific experiences or relationships that bring you joy. Your best friend. Your dog. Even something as simple as a crispy grilled cheese and a hot cup of tea. Picture that thing in your mind, and feel the pleasure it evokes. Now imagine your life no longer including that thing, and consider the pain its absence would inflict.

Negative visualization not only reminds us of what is important, it also demonstrates what is unimportant. When you are consciously grateful for your health, for your children's love, and for the sunshine that permits you to take a stress-reducing walk or jog, your brain will stop devoting excess energy to trivialities like the pile of dishes in your sink or that flaky co-worker who *still* hasn't returned your email.

When things feel dark, we must make an extra effort to appreciate what we still have left to enjoy. If you are reading this, you are alive. There's plenty of trouble in the world, but we are also surrounded by great beauty. It can sometimes be hard to appreciate, but there are meals to be savored, books to be read, and friends to be loved.

So wake up to the world's gifts. If you can learn to want what you already have, you'll realize that most of the things that bother you will pass. Even if you need a Gas-X to help speed up the process.

Life Is Short. Take a Swing.

What watching my kid play baseball taught me about life
MEDIUM, FEBRUARY 2021

"Never let the fear of striking out keep you from playing the game."
—*Babe Ruth*

Watching your child play baseball can be a highly stressful experience, especially when they get up to bat. Your pulse soars and hands tense as you wonder whether they'll triumph or return to the dugout in defeat.

Last season, my parental nerves grew increasingly agitated when my son adopted the strategy of "not swinging," in hopes of earning a walk. While it often worked, his coach pushed him to be more aggressive so he could gain the confidence that comes from making solid contact. The goal of Little League, of course, isn't just to get to first base or even to score a run.

Amidst the craziness of 2020, youth baseball gave my son and his teammates a safe environment to learn one of life's most important lessons: to achieve your potential, you have to take some risks.

One day, as I was watching the game from the dugout where I was helping with the equipment, my angst reached an apex. My son had just taken his sixth pitch, strike three. In an undisciplined moment, I growled "Swing the fucking bat!" just loud enough for one of his teammates to hear it.

"What did you say?" the kid asked, his expression surprised but delighted.

"I said, 'swing the freaking bat,'" I lied.

"That's not what I heard," he replied with a conspiratorial smile.

"Well, if he doesn't take a chance in baseball, he won't do it in other areas of his life that are far more important!"

The kid just looked at me and walked away, leaving me to reflect on my frayed emotions. In that moment, I realized my ambitions for my son were a projection of my own insecurities. While I thought I had implored him to take an actual rip at a literal baseball, I was really begging him not to follow in my footsteps. Inside, I was screaming, "My biggest regrets in life are the chances I didn't take!"

There was this girl I was in love with for most of high school. I harbored a painful, heart-pounding-out-of-my-sweater-vest teen crush on her, and I'm almost sure it was reciprocated. She gave me every positive signal short of screaming, "Kiss me, you moron!" But I never summoned the courage to make a move.

Then there was a blocked punt, deep in our archrival's end of the football field. All I had to do was pick it up and run 12 open yards to clinch our victory. I fell on it. We, the five-touchdown underdogs, got the ball back but failed to convert and lost the game.

This abundance of caution has probably spared me a lot of chaos in other areas of my life. Still, I have come to believe in the importance of not just seizing opportunity, but seeking it out, even when it's risky. Salespeople can't close big deals if they don't call the big client. Chefs or bakers can't learn new cuisine without tempting a blown recipe. And no one runs a marathon or writes a novel without putting themselves at risk of falling on their face.

The imperative to act boldly grows more critical with age. For a year after my mom died, my grieving, 87-year-old father had to force himself to get out of his apartment and socialize with the other residents of his senior home. One day, I found motivational notes he had written to himself, withered penmanship listing names of people to call and self-motivational tidbits like, "Be the one who reaches out," and, "Beat loneliness."

My dad could have given up, but he didn't. Alone for the first time since the 1950s, he carried on with courage and breathtaking grace for another six years, a ferociously sound mind pushing a brittle body out the door and onto the field of life.

If my beautiful boy has learned anything from my courageous father, I hope it's that: to live your best life, you've got to take some chances. Putting yourself out there invites rejection and failure. But doing so is the only way to throw open the doors of opportunity and achievement. Each of us gets a finite number of trips to the plate, and today is one of them. Swing the fucking bat.

Nightmare on the Back Nine

Dreams of stagnation are the scariest dreams of all
SUBSTACK, AUGUST 2023

The dream is always the same. I'm on the golf course, on a random tee box, somewhere in the middle of the round. I can't identify my playing partners, but they seem to be friends. Each of the three hits their shot and moves to the side.

It's my turn. I peg my tee in the ground. It topples over. I try again. It falls. I attempt the simple task with a different, longer tee. Same result. This happens several times. There is no wind, and I'm not encumbered by booze or other intoxicants. I just can't get the ball to stay put.

Maybe it's the club. I slide my driver back into the bag, but it falls down. Picking it up, I fumble with some irons, but eventually settle for my 3-wood. I return to the teeing ground where my friends have their bags slung over their shoulders, shuffling their feet and trading inquisitive, impatient glances.

There is nothing complicated about this shot—it is as straightforward as they come. But I never actually swing the club. I see the ball. I address the ball. I have every intent to hit the ball, but my arms are frozen. I try to turn my shoulders. Nothing happens.

The group ahead of us shrinks in the distance, and a log jam forms behind us. Etiquette now trumping indulgence, the balance of my foursome moves slowly forward in the direction of their drives. They say nothing and take a wide berth in the unlikely case I reach the fairway.

The scenario—me, alone on the tee, unable to move—continues, then dissolves inconclusively into blackness. There are no monsters or weapons or evil men chasing me—just the horrifying ordeal of being left behind, frozen and impotent.

Some people might interpret this vision with the knee-jerk response, "Oh, your nightmare is not being able to play golf? Your life is so difficult!" Such an assessment, of course, would miss the point on a couple of levels. First, sucking at golf is not my nightmare. That's my stark, waking reality. Second, even though every round offers countless ways to be frustrated and humiliated, I think the dream has little to do with the sport itself.

To find the underlying meaning, I googled "Dreams about being stuck," which offered few answers but reminded me that people who write about our slumbering minds on the internet also weave 99% of the dream-catchers for sale in Santa Fe. So I decided to do my own analysis.

My nightmare, which—it bears pointing out—I did not choose, is being trapped in some existential paralysis and not being able to move forward or being forgotten because I couldn't keep up. Or being too stubborn or dumb to let go of my personal Sisyphean tasks and change course.

Freud might ask, "Did your mother play golf and/or ever lock you in a broom closet?" To which I would answer, "No, and leave my mother out of this!" But giving psychoanalysis its due, I wonder to what degree being the 3rd boy and 5th out of six kids might have ingrained some fear of not being included by the older kids. Add to birth order issues the undeniable social pressure to achieve, and no wonder this kind of anxiety haunts my sleep.

Then there are the obvious overtones of death. Yes, it's a little cliché, but at least my brain didn't outfit the head pro in a hooded Peter Millar cloak and a scythe in the shape of a 1-iron.

Come to think of it, maybe the dream is about golf, or the sport as a metaphor for striving in life. Consider the role of agency in golf: a player endeavors to cause a small, dimpled sphere to travel a certain distance and direction across a field rife with obstacles and undulations. The more she plays, the more consistent the connection between her objective and her results, but there is always room for improvement.

Like self-actualization—the teeny triangle at the top of Maslow's Hierarchy—perfection in golf is never attained, only pursued. Shitty golfers like me keep playing not because we expect to achieve greatness but because the game offers fleeting glimpses of proficiency in which we cause the ball to fly the way we want it to fly. This temporary but transcendent alignment of intent and outcome lures us back to the course and, occasionally, even motivates us to practice.

No one is perfect, but persistence matters. In the 2023 (British) Open Championship, Brian Harman *smoked* the rest of the field, winning by six strokes over the runners-up, but still carded three bogeys in Sunday's final, rainy round. Of course, he also managed to grind out four birdies in that Liverpudlian deluge, demonstrating that victory is often more about tenacity than perfection.

In golf, as in life, you strive, and you fail. You make progress, then you fall back a little. You lose way more often than you win, but you keep playing because you love it, even when you suck. Hell isn't chunking your 80-yard approach shot into the lake, though that will make you curse all you previously held as sacred. Hell is being locked out of the game and being unable to play, which will happen to all of us eventually.

The only thing within our power is to get in as many rounds as possible and do our best to go down swinging.

The Sunk Cost of Thanksgiving Leftovers

After all we've been taught, is waste actually a sin?
SUBSTACK, DECEMBER 2023

Last Saturday morning, I found myself staring into the refrigerator at 2.5 leftover pies, a delicious collection of slightly picked-over pecan, pumpkin, and Dutch apple.

I love pie. Pie is good. But my wife and kids do not share my obsession, so the destiny of this post-Thanksgiving bounty lay solely in my hands.

Right behind me were a trash can and an in-sink disposal, either of which would have provided an appropriate resolution for these leftovers. After all, the holiday was done and it was time to resume normal nutritional practices, which do not include dessert after breakfast. But there's dietary prudence, and there are the voices in my head.

"Throwing these away would be wasteful," I thought. "And as we all know, waste is a sin!"

When you're raised Catholic by Depression-era parents, you accept these kinds of concepts about money and doctrine as self-evident truths. There's nothing more thoughtlessly wasteful—to say nothing of sinful—than throwing away food. Except masturbation.

The underlying fallacy of course comes from how we define "waste." In this case, it's helpful to remember the economic concept of sunk cost, i.e., an expense that has already been incurred, cannot be recovered, and thus should not be considered in evaluating future decisions.

Applied here, it means that the money exchanged for those pies is gone, so the only question to consider should be, "Is it a good idea to eat two and a half pies within a very short period of time?" In which case, one might consider other criteria, including both your undeniably expanding waistline and rapidly slowing metabolism.

As a parent, it's hardly the first time I have faced this dilemma. When my kids were little, I would voluntarily consume expired Dora the Explorer yogurts and freezer-burned, gluten-free corndogs instead of tossing them in the garbage. One morning, I nibbled one of said corndogs while driving through the carpool line at my kids' school. The teacher who opened the door for my then-kindergartners looked at me as if I was chugging a bottle of Jack Daniels. Dogs of corn, her judgy glare implied, should be eaten only by ex-convicts at state fairs and only after 11:00 a.m. I smiled, pointed at the previously ice-speckled meat stick, and announced, "It's gluten-free!" as if that explained anything.

What I was trying to say was that the kids won't eat them, so I have to. This raises the logical question as to why the GF options were bought in the first place, given that no one in our house has a celiac allergy. We'll address that rhetorical, passive-voice question some other time.

As my kids got older, the need to teach them food-based thrift intensified. When they were 9 and 10, we went with another family to one of those high-end steak houses where my 54-pound daughter ordered a $54 filet—a la carte, natch—and ate maybe 17% of it.

Having worked at several high-end restaurants in my early adulthood, I know that there is little chance the meat would have ended up in the trash. The "bus tub buffet" is a real thing that occurs in restaurant kitchens, augmenting the meager income of waiters, busboys, and dishwashers. Yes, I have eaten discarded treats off of strangers' plates countless times. I know my daughter's entree won't be "wasted," but that happens behind the scenes and I want my kids to *see* the connection between what they order and what they consume. So you bet your ass I had them box up that steak, along with the leftover sides of creamed spinach and onion rings.

This ethical stand comes at a cost. Not only do I occasionally embarrass my wife and our friends by walking out of a 5-star restaurant with a doggie bag, but because I cannot consider my kids' half-eaten cheeseburgers, French dips, or fries as the sunk costs that they are, those morsels end up in my belly instead of in the compost where they belong. On one hand, I'm demonstrating financial accountability. On the other hand, I am carrying around an extra 12 pounds of belly fat—and God knows how much arterial plaque—to prove this point.

Maybe it's the diluted blood of a famished Irish "green mouth" ancestor who died after eating grass or maybe it's the combination of frugality and the fear of hell. But there's a weird thought I have when I see a fully stocked refrigerator. Instead of thinking, "We are so lucky to have all this," I think, "Let's finish that up before it spoils."

Which brings me back to the pie. If there's a sin here, it's how much we bought in the first place, but that doesn't occur to me as I evaluate my choices. Eating the apple was easy enough to justify. It's apples, for God's sake! Since pecans have lots of protein, that's good for muscles, and well, who doesn't love pumpkin? It's from a gourd, so it's gotta be wholesome, right?

Fueled by hunger as much by virtue and these specious rationalizations, I devoured those pies. Okay, I did not eat *all* two-and-a-half—I scooped out some of the filling and threw away a good bit of crust. But conservatively speaking, I ate a solid 1.75 pies over the next 30 hours.

And I did it because it was the right thing to do.

Staying Hungry When Your Life is Full

What the scale is really telling us
SUBSTACK, APRIL 18 2023

I weighed in this morning at 224.5 lbs. It's the heaviest I've been since I lost the sympathy weight after our first child was born.

Last time, my heft resulted from a back injury, lots of business travel, and the cupcakes my pregnant wife would bring to the office. I was pudgy—like Ned Beatty in *Deliverance* soft (and we know what happened to him). I'm much stronger now, but the scale reveals the inconvenient truth that my biceps, triceps, and glutes are Wagyu-caliber marbled.

It's all diet, and I know it. I work out with a trainer on Mondays and Thursdays and I walk at least 15 miles per week. But what, when, and how I eat breaks all the rules. Oddly, it's me living my dream that causes this fitness challenge.

If you work a 9:00-5:00 job, you can mostly digest your dinner before you nestle down. But my schedule is staggered five hours to the right. To even stay awake for comedy shows past 10:00 p.m., I drink a cup of coffee at 3:00 in the afternoon. After the show, I'm totally wired and nowhere near ready for bed. When I get home, there's a pan of brownies on the counter, leftover pot pie in the fridge, and an open bottle of red wine begging me to finish it off. Who am I to resist?

So I jam 1,200 calories down my gullet at 11:30 p.m. then watch *Golf Central* and fall asleep on the couch. An hour later, I'll brush my teeth, get in bed, and set the alarm for 6:15 a.m. so I can wake the kids up. At which point, I'll slam three cups of coffee to get myself going.

Coffee up, cabernet down. I'm like a preppy Elvis, and it's starting to show.

This weight gain is actually an indication of how lucky I am. I'm doing exactly what I want in life, if maybe not quite at the level I'd like to be doing it. I make audiences laugh then return to a beautiful home where my wife is in bed sleeping with the dog and my two healthy children are snuggled in upstairs. I can't imagine not doing both comedy and parenting at full speed.

But fuck, man.

I think my body is a metaphor for life in the primo zip codes. Last year, I said no to a half-dozen golf or ski trips: Vail, Bandon Dunes, Ireland, etc. It's not that I don't want to go—I love to golf and I love to ski. But if that's all you do, that's all you'll be good at. As worthy and healthy as these pursuits might be, they're not what I feel called to work on.

In a world of opulent distractions, I'm trying to stay hungry. Why? Ernest Becker, author of *The Denial of Death* might suggest that I'm striving for immortality. The pursuit to play bigger rooms or get millions of people to listen to my podcast, he would argue, is an attempt to prove, when I go, not only that I existed but that I *mattered*.

This is certainly true on some level and part of the "dignified madness" that makes us uniquely human. Within a generation or two, 99.9% of us will exist only as diluted DNA in the double-helices of our great-grandchildren, if that. We know this, if only subconsciously, and we fight it every day.

But I honestly think it's something else also—not just a futile pursuit of immortality but the genuine embrace of mortality. The opportunity to be who we want to be is right here, right now, and there's no guarantee it will be available tomorrow (kind of like the leftovers in the fridge). So whether there are 30 or 3,000 people in the audience, the impetus is the same. Still, my life will not mean more if I get famous or if my podcast finally gets the recognition it so richly deserves.

Why not stop and smell the flowers then? Well, this *is* smelling the flowers. The whole reason I chose this path was to avoid the deathbed remorse of wondering "what if I had given the creative life a full swing?" or regretting that I had not been a better dad or husband.

The pursuit matters. My kids will never be this age again and as porky as I am right now—hopefully temporarily—I will never be this young or healthy again. So I'm gathering rosebuds, I'm busy being born, and all that shit. Like Frost in the snowy woods, I have promises to keep and miles to go before I sleep.

But before I go to bed, I think I'll finish the rest of that pot pie.

Stop Keeping Score

How to quit measuring success by net
worth, fancy titles, or TikTok views

MEDIUM, NOVEMBER 2020

A few years ago, when I was looking for a new workout routine, my wife suggested I take a spin class at a place called Flywheel. The last time I had biked en masse was at a fancy California health club, so Flywheel's spandexed clientele, neon lighting, and ebullient instructor were not new to me. But one thing did stand out: behind the coach hung a flat-panel screen displaying each rider's name, bike number, and total "power points." It was a scoreboard.

Giving it little thought, I spent the next 45 minutes just trying to follow the leader's directions. But that first session ended with my pulse racing, my t-shirt dripping, and my name near the bottom of the list. Over subsequent classes, I became obsessed with moving up.

Eventually, I cracked the code: to score high, one had to pick one of the "fast" bikes, ignore the instructor, and do nothing but pedal like crazy. The scoreboard soon replaced the fitness benefits as my main driver. Thirty seconds into a ride, I'd see "CycleFella" rise above "PaulO69," and think, "Not today, CycleFella!" Then I'd spend the rest of class proving that I was better than the guy, even on days when my body was begging me to take it easy.

The whole experience reminded me of how scoreboards drive our behavior in many other areas of our lives. Even though Teddy Roosevelt reminded us that "comparison is the thief of joy," consciously or not, we design our days around improving our positions on invisible career ladders that supposedly quantify success. When I was a kid, I'd throw a fit if one of my siblings got a bigger piece of cake than I did. Today, I look in the neighbor's driveway and can't help but evaluate my life based in part on what I see parked there.

Escaping this pattern isn't easy, but it can be done. On a recent episode of my podcast, I spoke with Yoshee and Diana Sodiq, the hosts of their own podcast about intentional living called *F the Joneses*. Years ago, Yoshee's work as a consultant and Diana's as a doctor had earned them fancy cars and a big house with a pool, but they both yearned to do something more creative with their careers. They realized they had spent years trying to "keep up with the Joneses," and that while they'd reached the spot on the ladder that they thought would bring them happiness, the life they'd created just wasn't working for them. As Yoshee told me, "One day, we decided, 'eff the Joneses.'" They traded Diana's Mercedes SUV for a Honda minivan, moved into a smaller home, and began living on their own terms.

For Yoshee, the most important part of the process of taking control was "defining who we are," he told me. It's a critical insight. We define who we are by picking—or not picking—the metrics we use to assign value. Left to their own devices, our brains will measure success by our net worth or TikTok views because those things are far easier to quantify than the amount of creativity, joy, and connection we experience every day.

Try this: instead of counting the number of friends you have on Facebook, count the number of meaningful conversations you've had in real time this month. Rather than comparing your results against your neighbor's efforts, set a personal goal, and track your performance over time. People may judge your decisions. "It's human nature," Diana said on a recent episode of *F the Joneses*. "But guess what? It has nothing to do with you."

Rather than relentlessly grinding out in your fancy spin class, maybe it would be more satisfying for you to pedal to the beat of the music. Or better yet, take your bike outside and cruise around with the people you love. Your name might not end up at the top of a leaderboard, but finishing first is not the same as having enjoyed the ride.

Don't Take a Break from Social Media. Manage It.

As someone who recently checked my phone 1,000 times in a week, I'm finally learning how

MEDIUM, MAY 2020

A couple weeks ago, as I stared vacantly into my phone, my wife offered a gentle observation about the amount of screen time I'd been consuming. Her kind implication: I was spending too much time on Facebook.

"Honey," I replied, "it's no big deal—I'm just checking to see if anybody outside of our house remembers that I'm still alive."

She sighed, patted me on the head, then walked into the other room.

Alone with my thoughts and my mobile lifeline to the rest of the planet, I tried to assure myself I was only joking. But my words contained an ugly and undeniable truth: even as I'm quarantining with my wife and two kids—the people I love most—I am starving for human connection. The numbers supported her observation, however. According to Apple's Screen Time report, I had picked up my phone almost one thousand times the previous week.

Look, I'm all for cutting ourselves a break, which was a positive side effect of quarantining during Covid, but this is not the behavior of someone practicing self-kindness! This is a cry for help. Like an over-caffeinated Eleanor Rigby, I've been compulsively grabbing my phone and tapping blue logos in the hope that someone on the other side would say to me:

"I see you."

"I miss you."

"You have a great nose."

I am by no means hating on social media. Full disclosure: I am very proud to have worked at Facebook for several years. It's also important to remember that Facebook is neither inherently good nor evil (though the company has rightly fallen under scrutiny for how it handles privacy and the distribution of misleading information). Ultimately, it is how we use the platform—and social media in general—that determines whether it creates a net benefit or detriment to our lives.

Every game, ride-sharing, news, e-commerce, and music app on our phone is designed to entice us into returning as often as possible for a quick fix of brain feelies (aka dopamine). LinkedIn's "Who Viewed Your Profile?" feature is crack for narcissists. Once, when LinkedIn was experiencing a technical glitch, the site informed me that "No one has looked at your profile in the past 90 days." For a brief moment, I thought I had died. Even my meditation app prods me to post inspirational quotes after each session, which seems like the exact opposite of what meditation is supposed to be about.

If we don't consciously choose how and why we interact with these products, we permit them to turn our days into long bouts of slack-jawed navel-gazing. And that's the problem: as useful and fun as social media can be, a quarantine is absolutely the wrong time to abdicate your mood and self-worth to an algorithm. Now more than ever, we need the nourishment of human connection, yet social media delivers all the nutrition of a TikTok—I mean a Tic Tac.

In one episode of my podcast, I asked Laura Delizonna, PhD, a Stanford instructor and expert on the science of happiness, how we can protect ourselves from self-defeating behavior while sheltering in place. She answered by citing the work of psychiatrist and concentration camp-survivor Viktor Frankl: "Between a stimulus and a response is a space, and in that space, we have the power to choose our response." That moment is our opportunity to make the healthy choice, but to do that, Delizonna pointed out, it's important "to pause and to notice that you do have a choice to get off autopilot." We have the power to pick up an apple instead of a bag of Cool Ranch Doritos. To pour a virgin spritzer instead of another vodka tonic. To pat your husband on the head instead of calling him a "hopeless digital junkie."

In other words, the best way to deal with feelings of isolation is to strike a healthy balance. I'm not quitting Facebook or the other social media platforms any time soon, but I am trying to recognize the moments of choice Delizonna mentions. I have picked up my phone 13% fewer times in recent weeks. It's still too much, but I'm improving.

If you'd like to reduce the amount of time you spend gazing at your mobile, consider these steps:

- **Turn off notifications.** The more you can avoid the temptation to dive into the vortex of apps, the more time you'll have for life-affirming activities like exercising, reading, or talking to another person in real time.
- **Acknowledge and pause.** When you feel the urge to engage in some digital grazing, recognize this as either a genuine desire to connect or a dopamine craving for which there are some really good alternatives.
- **Replace the suboptimal behavior with something healthier.** You can still pick up your phone, but instead of surfing the socials, click on "Contacts" and go old-school: make a phone call. Or seize the moment to organize a virtual happy hour. I was very skeptical about this concept at first, but have found these gatherings far more gratifying than I imagined. I still can't fist bump my buddies or punch them in their dumb shoulders, but Zoom's droplet-free interface delivers smiles, laughter, or even shared tears if that's what the situation calls for.

You're not going to get this right at first or even after many attempts, and that's okay. Now is no time to beat yourself up for not being perfect. But if you practice the process of acknowledging, pausing, and replacing, you can still use social media without letting it run your life.

Because you are alive, you do matter, and you really do have a terrific nose.

You Deserve It!

Or maybe you don't, but that's not the point
SUBSTACK, MARCH 2023

In the climactic scene of the 1992 western, Unforgiven, William Munny (played by Clint Eastwood) holds a rifle to the chest of a supine and wounded Little Bill Daggett (Gene Hackman), the corrupt sheriff who had tortured and killed Munny's friend and partner. Little Bill looks up from the floor and pleads his case. "I don't deserve this—to die like this. I was building a house."

For almost two hours, the film's tension has built to the confrontation between these two legendary actors, and Munny's simple reply proves every bit as powerful as the muzzle blast that follows.

With a classic Eastwood growl, Munny answers Little Bill: "*Deserve's* got nothing to do with it."

I think about this scene all the time. You'd expect Munny to point out that Little Bill, after the horrible acts he has committed, *totally* deserves what's coming to him. Instead, he delivers a profound insight into a fallacy of human logic: the disinterested universe cares little for the concept of deservingness or the plans we're making, no matter how much we believe it should.

Before I write much more, I'll acknowledge that this is a massive, complex topic, and I won't pretend to solve the issues of fairness, meritocracy, or nepo babies in a 1,016-word essay. But I have one goal here—to ask that when you hear someone using any form of the infinitive "to deserve," you stop and consider what's behind the words.

When I say, "I deserve this!" it usually implies a degree of entitlement—as if either my work ethic or charming personality merits the outcome I desire. If I say, "She doesn't deserve that," in reference to something I want but do not have, my words invariably reflect underlying resentment, envy, or pettiness.

The human tendency to think in these terms goes way back. The Gospels grapple with deservingness in the parables of the prodigal son and of the vineyard workers. In both cases, individuals who didn't do the work or play by the rules still earn a full reward, which understandably pisses off those who put in the time.

It's especially hard for us to deal with this kind of "unfairness" in zero-sum situations like college admissions. Last spring, my friend's daughter got into a top university—let's call it Princeton—because the soccer coach needed a goalkeeper. My friend's child had a solid academic record but more relevantly, she happened to play the right position in the right sport at the right time. Did she *deserve* to beat out 22 other very qualified applicants for that spot? I don't know—does Pete Davidson *deserve* to have sex with Emily Ratajkowski?

It's just how life works. Opportunities don't always accrue based on grades, test scores, or inherent virtue. And to be clear here, I'm not writing off persisting societal issues that prevent people from obtaining opportunities due to their race, gender, etc. I'm talking about the fact that luck, randomness, or life circumstances intervene in ways that appear contrary to the way the world, from our limited, self-centered human perspective, "ought" to work.

It's the same with money. Wealth often finds people who didn't "earn" it, via inheritance, alimony, or dumb luck. Do they deserve it? Wrong question. The right question is, "so what?" They have it and they'll probably keep it. If that bothers me, well, that's my problem.

In this kind of situation, it's helpful to remind myself that I already have so much that I personally didn't earn. Did I *deserve* to be born to two parents who loved, protected, and educated me in the wealthiest country in history during a time of peace and stability? Clearly, I did nothing to justify such a solid foundation, but it eventually paid off financially. Of course, I could have had those same privileges and decided to slack off—my calculus homework didn't do itself, after all. In any case, even though my last name isn't Carnegie or Kardashian, I still won the genetic lottery.

Also, we should remember that the concept of deservingness works the other way too. This year, over 600,000 Americans will die from cancer. They were busy living their lives—raising children, building houses like Little Bill—when the universe stepped in and dealt them cards they did not deserve.

Oh sure, you can increase the odds of staying healthy by eating right and exercising—and you can't win Powerball if you don't play—but these outcomes are mostly the products of the universe's incomprehensible, indifferent math. *Deserve's* got nothing to do with it.

Still, while keeping Munny's words in mind, it might be helpful to ponder the literal definition of "deserve," i.e., to be worthy of a thing. If, through luck or effort, you have something others want, here are some ways you can be worthy of it:

- **Be grateful.** First and last, practice gratitude for your good fortune. As hard as "self-made" people may have worked and as much as they may have delayed gratification, all of us have had help or gotten lucky along the way.
- **Be prudent.** A good steward takes care of her assets. She is not reckless with them and honors them by not exposing them to unnecessary risk. As Warren Buffett says, "It's insane to risk what you have and need for something you don't need."
- **Be generous.** If nobody deserves anything, you can honor your bounty by sharing it, if only because your generosity serves you as well as others. In their book *Happy Money*, researchers Mike Norton and Liz Dunn report that giving to charity had the same happiness-boosting effect as a doubling of income.
- **Be self-aware.** You've gotten so many opportunities *just because*. You've avoided calamity and disease mostly out of good luck. Never forget that—because it's temporary.

Beware of thinking in the "deserve" binary. It's not helpful and it cuts both ways. One of these days, while you're out there living your life, the ball of good fortune will bounce your way. Or, an oncoming truck will swerve into your lane.

You don't *deserve* either. But even if you did, it wouldn't change the outcome.

Why Marriage is Hard

The upside to being known
SUBSTACK, MARCH 2024

> "If we want the rewards of being loved, we have to submit to the mortifying ordeal of being known"
> —*Tim Kreider, New York Times*

"My God, would you please stop picking your lip." Over the past few years, my wife has said this to me at least 172 times.

My lip sometimes cracks and I pick at it. It's a disgusting habit—something I do, presumably, to soothe my low-grade but persistent anxiety. Whatever the reason, I acknowledge that it's a nasty habit, but it still irritates me when she points it out.

The myriad incidents where she sees my weaknesses lead me to believe that the hardest part of marriage isn't dealing with your partner's faults, though that can certainly be challenging. The hardest part is seeing your imperfection through their omnipresent, sometimes judgy eyes and understanding that—no matter what—you cannot hide from them. This is the "mortifying ordeal of being known," as Tim Kreider refers to it in the above epigraph.

Consciously or not, we spend our teenage and early adult years rationalizing our imperfections so we can see our reflection without throwing up. Through denial and rationalization, we weave a narrative shell that makes our foibles, large and small, seem normal or even virtuous:

- I'm anxious because I was raised Catholic.
- I'm overweight because I'm not caught up in shallow body stereotypes.
- I cried during *Wicked* because I have the soul of an artist.

Sure you do.

While each of these might hold a nugget of truth, they are tales we construct to protect our delicate egos. They work as long as we keep the world at arm's length, not letting anyone close enough to see what's really going on.

But then you get married. What you get, in addition to a lover, co-parent, and partner in taking on the world, is a full-time, 24/7/365 observer and occasional commentator on your life. Basically, you get someone who knows you better than you know yourself, who doesn't have the carefully crafted excuse-machine in which you've wrapped your inadequacy. And that is awful scary because while you can bullshit yourself, you cannot bullshit your spouse.

Your siblings, if you have any, know you up to a certain extent. They saw you pee your pants in the school play, knew you cheated on a test in seventh grade, and witnessed you sneak champagne at your cousin's wedding, then eat coleslaw with your drunken hands before you barfed in the bushes (btw, who serves coleslaw at a wedding?). You, likewise, have the goods on them—so you're charitable to each other, if only because you share the same genetic flaws.

But your spouse has the current data.

He or she's going to learn that, deep down, you are still a petrified child who craves the love of a distant mother, or you're scared of abandonment, or desperate to be acknowledged by the world. They will see that, even if you're a pretty good person who values honesty, on some level you are a spineless hypocrite just like everyone else.

You will beseech your partner, "Avert your eyes from my hideous countenance!" But they can't. They're there—every single day, with a front-row seat to the carnival shit show that is your life.

In Justin Timberlake's song "Mirrors," he sings about his hot wife, Jessica Biel. "It's like you're my mirror, my mirror staring back at me." It's supposed to be romantic, but I find it petrifying. When I see certain aspects of myself reflected through my wife's eyes, I'm revolted. It's like how comedian Doug Stanhope expresses his reaction when he sees his aging face in the mirror: "That can't be right."

Being known is indeed a mortifying ordeal. While it's relatively easy to forgive others for their imperfections, it requires trust that they will also forgive you for yours. When someone accepts you for all of you, that love can be hard to embrace.

But said acceptance has profound benefits. A few months back, Stacey said to me, "What's happening with your lip isn't normal. You should have a doctor look at it." So I did. The dermatologist prescribed an antibiotic ointment that knocked out the lip-cracking right away. Unfortunately, it returned a few weeks later.

On a subsequent visit, she cut a chunk of my lip off and ordered a biopsy. The test showed the presence of serious sun damage and pre-cancerous cells, which she proceeded to burn off with liquid nitrogen.

Holy crap! I could have gotten squamous cell carcinoma on my lip. That would have been ugly at best, and fatal at worst. And I probably never would have gone to the doctor unless my wife saw what I was unwilling to admit to myself.

Yes, being known is mortifying, but it might just save your life.

The Future is Analog: Learn to Fight

Rich people aren't ready for the apocalypse

SUBSTACK, FEBRUARY 2023

The most disturbing moment of the pandemic for me was the day I realized those doomsday survivalist folks might not be so crazy after all. Sometime in May 2020, barely getting by in a world with air conditioning, wi-fi, and Uber Eats, it dawned on me: I probably wouldn't do so great in a post-apocalyptic world. And after catching up on HBO's 2023 hit, The Last of Us, I'm convinced of my future worthlessness.

For decades, I have thrived in the game of business and life, taking for granted the Rule of Law, stable infrastructure, and a functioning electrical grid on which the game board teeters. Meanwhile, I regarded people who stockpile kerosene, canned beans, and shotgun shells in their storm cellars with—let's be honest—smug superiority.

If you bet that the housing market was going to melt down in 2005, you paid a dear price. Your analysis of market dynamics might have been dead-on, but your timing cost you a fortune. On the other hand, those who wagered on a 2008 collapse made billions. The market was always going to fall apart—it was just a matter of time.

In a similar manner, doomsday preppers aren't wrong—they're just early. So far. The chance of our collective demise in any one year is a low-odds bet, but over the long run, it's inevitable. In recent history, the arch of the universe has bent toward justice. Eventually, it will bend back toward anarchy. So as the locusts swarm, the preppers are going to retreat to their lairs, lock their gates, and leave the rest of us begging for entry.

"Let me in," I'll plead, "I went to Dartmouth!"

"Sorry pal," the preppers will say, standing like Noah in newly formed puddles on the deck of his ark, "we tried to tell you."

What got us into the 1%, or reasonably close to it, will not sustain us in this new economy, and there will be precious little time to retrain. Learn to code? Don't make me laugh. The future, my friends, is analog. So learn to fight. Learn to skin a buck, to run a trotline, and—while the internet is still a thing—take MacGyver's Masterclass because the next phase of society will require knowledge and craft they don't teach at Ivy League graduate schools.

When the grid collapses, so will disappear our recently embraced tendency to not murder and eat each other. We will form tribes, and I don't mean cute, Seth Godin-esque groups cohering around shared interests like pickleball or locally sourced cuisine. I'm talking about feral, *Walking Dead*-style packs of marauding savages fighting off rival gangs and zombies with fungi on the brain. We'll eat organic all right, but it won't be the farm-to-table variety. It's going to be the digging-in-the-dirt-for-a-juicy-grub, stalking-raccoons, and sucking-the-nutrients-out-of-tree-bark organic.

You might be thinking, "Paul, you shouldn't use the word 'tribes' because it's insensitive toward First Nations people." Thanks for proving my point. You know who doesn't care about modern language protocols? The governor of Dystopiaville, which is where we're all going to reside soon. When the Gov asks what skills you have to support the tribe, answers like "I'm a diversity consultant/investment banker/Instagram influencer" will land your head on a pike.

We, the current, temporary elite—progressives and conservatives alike—have gamed the prevailing system to extract maximum value for ourselves and our children. But we are also the most ill-prepared for this imminent new economy. Sure, Elon Musk has a luxury fall-out shelter in New Zealand, but do you?

If you're lucky you will empty bed pans. More likely, you will end up the involuntary courtesan to the Redneck Road Warriors who compose the new ruling class. Because in the coming labor market, there are only two jobs: fighters and fluffers. And nothing will put your modern anxieties, political distractions, and petty inconveniences into perspective like the hot breath of a Dothraki commando on the back of your neck.

No, I'm not beating the "we need a good war" drum. But whether we need it or not, it will find us eventually: a hard rain's gonna fall. The levee's gonna break. Winter is coming.

At some point, there will be a revolution, and those of us at the top will pay a very high price. Every day I don't learn Krav Maga or hydroponics, I'm increasing the odds against making it through the Apocalypse with my pretty mouth. But it probably won't happen in my lifetime.

See you on the golf course.

Your Neighbors Are Your World

If there's one thing the pandemic taught us, it's that life is local. Research from the World Happiness Report backs this up.

MEDIUM, DECEMBER 2020

A few years into my marriage, my young family relocated to my childhood hometown of Atlanta. After a couple of decades moving all over the country for a series of new schools or job opportunities, I felt it was time to pick a place and put down some roots.

But after several months back home, things weren't gelling socially quite the way I had hoped. So I called my former leadership coach, Alpesh Bhatt, and confessed that I just wasn't finding the community I had hoped to rediscover. Al, who seemed to know me well from the first day we met, sighed and reminded me, "My friend, one does not *find* community. One *creates* community."

He was, of course, right. I had been waiting for my new community to find me, but I had done little to reach out and assemble one of my own.

I thought of Al last week as I was speaking to John Helliwell on my podcast. Helliwell is the editor of the World Happiness Report (WHR), an annual study evaluating 156 countries by how well their citizens believe their lives are going. Given the downright scary issues facing us right now, I asked him, "What steps can I take to improve my happiness, assuming I can't move away or affect the structure of society?"

"Ahh, but you *can* affect the structure of your society!" Helliwell corrected with gentle clarity. "Because life is local."

Local? At first, I thought he was implying that I could better my community by doing something like running for the school board. Instead, he shared conclusions from WHR research, which showed that—given a basic level of societal stability—our individual contentment depends more on the quality and amount of interaction we have with friends, and less on macro-political or biological issues that are much further outside our scope of control.

Helliwell wasn't trying to give me a pep talk about how I have the power to change the lives of my 7 billion co-humans. He was simply saying that if each of us reaches out to a person down the street—even with something as simple as dropping off some fruit from your backyard or a package of Clorox wipes—we can create meaningful communities that enrich the lives of all involved.

"There is an infinite variety of things you can do with—or for—your neighbors," Helliwell told me. "It takes nothing more than a few steps and a few smiles to get the micro-connections going."

It's worth it to cultivate those micro-connections. The more introverted among us might need a little push to step and smile in the right direction, but the numbers, which come from annual Gallup World Poll data since 2012, clearly indicate that efforts to do so will pay off handsomely. Even a tedious activity like standing in line, which usually degrades our mood by a few percentage points, brightens our day when done with a friend. Taking a walk or a hike is a pretty reliable way to boost our disposition a little, but when strolling with someone else, according to the WHR, the benefit is four times greater.

And here's a fascinating insight: while taking a trip with a friend improves our day by an average of 5.3%, the beneficial effects are only 3.9% when road-tripping with a partner. I'm no statistician, but I'd guess your friend is more likely than your partner to agree on the shortest route, suitable driving music, and an agreeable cabin temperature.

Though we can't travel or gather in person right now, almost all of us could use more ties to our community. We need friends. We need our neighbors—especially now.

One might argue that a small percentage bump in attitude would do little to offset the upheaval of the pandemic. While Helliwell acknowledges the profound stress of unemployment and reduced incomes, he cites anecdotal evidence that reconnecting with our local communities boosts resilience in a meaningful way. He shared, "You ask people how they're doing and they say, 'I feel more connected to my neighborhood than I did before. And I'm meeting (neighbors) on the streets…and ditto with my friends, and we're even cooking at home.'"

So, take heart: during a bleak time, it's a comforting reminder that much of your happiness lies within your control.

But don't just heart, take the initiative. Instead of spending hours pondering what the world might impose on you, take a few minutes to consider what small acts of community you might unleash.

You don't need anyone's permission. When you view life as local, your block becomes your world.

Toilet Paper as Societal Barometer

What remains on the shelf tells us a lot about America
MEDIUM, MARCH 2020

Like most of the country, I went to the grocery store early in the pandemic to stock up on non-perishables for our pantry and freezer. Given warnings in the news and on Facebook, the lack of toilet paper on the shelves came as no surprise. Yet even though our friends and the media may have wanted us to see this TP deficit as a harbinger of societal collapse, other shelves in the store, with their plethora of convenient and comfortable toilet paper substitutes, suggested a different story.

I concluded that we should measure the extent of our societal collapse not by the media's or our friends' hysteria, but by the lengths to which we'll go to clean our backsides. Because the wide availability of rear-cleansing alternatives told me that we were merely playing at apocalypse. Until we are willing to endure the slightest bit of discomfort or exercise an iota of ingenuity to wipe our butts, we remain a very safe distance from a true crisis.

So before you waste any more mental energy worrying about the lack of tissue, please consider where we are on my TP Defcon Scale. Modeled after the Pentagon's five-tiered defense readiness condition system, TPDS will give you plenty of warning before the poop hits the fan.

TP DEFCON 1: This Ain't No Crisis (Kleenex/Moist wipes)

Here's where we are as a culture: shoppers brawl over toilet paper on aisle 4, while fifteen feet away, dozens of boxes of downy soft Kleenex sit patiently, waiting to be taken home. Clearly, we are a lazy, unimaginative people, prone more to outrage than to adaptation.

Raise your hand if you've ever wiped with a Kleenex. (Please note: you're raising your hand.) Did it feel as if the world was ending? Of course not. Maybe you double or triple-folded, but you didn't give it a second thought. And Kleenex was just the beginning. My local Kroger also had in full supply the moistened, flushable butt wipes preferred by some children and those who equate corporeal cleanliness with godliness, i.e., me. If you've never tried these, I beg you to treat yourself. Follow a Kleenex with one of these delightful towelettes for a five-star, pre-dystopian, tush-cleaning experience your grandparents could have only dreamed about.

It's not just effective—it's downright refreshing. You know how your teeth feel when you leave the dentist? Well, I think I'll just leave it there.

TP DEFCON 2: No Big Deal. (Napkins: regular and cocktail)

If people are hoarding toilet paper but haven't even thought to buy table napkins instead, nothing material in our world has changed. TV prognosticators scream "HURRICANE!!!" when, at worst, it's "partly cloudy."

At our area Target, *tens of thousands* of perfectly adequate table napkins lingered unacknowledged. This is the same product that 90% of fraternity houses use as their preferred TP 50 weeks per year (with exceptions made for homecoming and parents weekend). So, it was fine when you were an undergrad, but now using them constitutes nuclear winter? Come on.

Let's say you can't find any of these table napkins and you have to go to TP Defcon 2b. Still not a problem, as the typical suburban home contains weeks' worth of back-up TP in the form of random birthday, seasonal, and cocktail napkins featuring boozy witticisms like:

"Rosé all day?"

"It's 5:00 somewhere!"

"Between us, Mommy's half buzzed."

They're not Charmin-soft, but think of how kitschy it will be to swab your caboose with a napkin embossed with a subtle wink to entry-level alcoholism. Hilarious, right!?!

DEFCON 2c: Don't forget those cutlery packets you get from restaurants when you order takeout or delivery. You likely have dozens of these environmental nightmares loitering pointlessly in some kitchen drawer or cabinet. What do you see cohabitating with those plastic sporks and the salt/pepper? Toilet paper!

TP DEFCON 3: Going South. (Coffee filters/Dryer Sheets)

I'm not saying the Corona Virus vacation couldn't get scary. It sure could. But we're not even close to the precipice until you find yourself looking at a Mr. Coffee coffee filter and thinking, "That would get the job done."

The process wouldn't kill you, but it's a sure sign the waters have gotten choppy.

Dryer sheets are another practical if unappealing option. The first time will be scary because you won't know if the fabric softener will cause a rash. But if you can get away with it, there are worse things than a behind that smells like tulips until the CDC gives the all-clear.

TP DEFCON 4: Getting Bad. (Lunch bags/doilies)

Now it's getting real. Previous generations have endured far worse in the form of depressions, plagues, and global wars, but still, if you're dredging your netherworld with a brown paper bag and that's your least-bad option, life's heading in the wrong direction.

Alternatives to this unforgiving sandwich transporter include items previously considered sacred, or at least non-disposable. So as you stare into the face of both apocalypse and once-in-a-lifetime hemorrhoids, you realize you have no higher use for those linen napkins or Grandma's antique lace doilies. Sure, you'll be sullying an heirloom, but you haven't used them since she died anyway.

TP DEFCON 5: Run for the Hills!
(U.S. Currency/Stock Certificates)

Board up your home and head for the mountains, because once you consider using financial assets for personal hygiene, winter is no longer "coming"—it has arrived.

Don't freak out too early, however. While corporate equities hold 30% less value than they did a couple of weeks ago, there is a long way to go before they're worthless.

With regard to currency—they say money is just a concept based on trust, and once that trust is gone, cash is worth no more than the paper it's printed on. But at least you have the option to use it as paper!

And here, my friends, is where traditional currency demonstrates its clear superiority over crypto. Because when Bitcoin goes to zero, you can't even use it to wipe your ass.

Want to Be Happier? Check the Thesaurus

The struggle to attain a deeply meaningful life may be an issue of language

MEDIUM, MARCH 2021

In all of my podcast interviews, I make a point of asking my guest how each of us can lead a happier life. Again and again, whether the interviewee is a best-selling author, prominent academic, or another sort of high achiever, the same answer keeps coming up: "Lower your expectations."

The first few times I heard this advice, I refused to accept it. "Low expectations" sounds defeatist. It sounds like giving up on happiness altogether. But over time, I've realized that the gap between their advice and how most of us think is an issue of language—specifically, it's an issue of conflicting interpretations of the word "happiness." To close that gap, we need to examine the term more closely.

Let's do a little exercise. On a piece of paper, draw a "happiness line" across the page. Write the word "sexy" on the far left of the line and "not so sexy" on the right (I promise this won't get weird). Now think of all the synonyms for "happiness" and plot them on the line.

As you write them down, you may notice that the left side is heavy on words like "jubilation," "bliss," and "euphoria," while the right side contains terms like "tranquility," "peace of mind," and "well-being."

While all these words indicate some kind of happiness, they imply wildly different forms of it. The latter group fits pretty closely with Aristotle's concept of *eudaimonia*, a word that has been translated as "fulfillment." The former group characterizes what comedian Dennis

Miller once described as "life in Heff's jacuzzi," in reference to the famed hot tub at the Playboy Mansion.

When my guests recommend lower expectations, they're not saying we should all give up or stop working hard to find happiness. I believe what they are advocating is choosing the right side of this happiness continuum—the side that's less about chasing highs, and more about keeping things steady.

Left-side happiness, while very exciting, is—at best—perishable. It might come from expensive toys or short-term companionship. You might feel it when your favorite team wins the Super Bowl or when you go viral on TikTok. But it dissipates as quickly as it arrives, and at worst, it beckons chaos into our lives. Fortunately or unfortunately, "sexy" doesn't scale.

Right-side happiness, by contrast, is an enduring state of mind that has to be earned. You cannot buy, rent, or borrow contentment. While decidedly unglamorous, it is a slow-burning, substantive condition that leaves us free of want and secure in our okay-ness. This doesn't disallow spontaneous moments of joy, but it eliminates the need to seek them out as a lifestyle. It also allows us to deal with whatever the world sends our way, which is key, because *resisting* life's imperfections and discomforts can become a major source of dissatisfaction.

The author and former *Guardian* columnist Oliver Burkeman, a two-time guest on my show, wrote in his book *The Antidote: Happiness for People who Can't Stand Positive Thinking*, "The effort to try to feel happy is often precisely the thing that makes us miserable. Our constant efforts to eliminate the negative—insecurity, uncertainty, failure, or sadness—that is what causes us to feel so insecure, anxious, uncertain, or unhappy."

Said slightly differently, lowering expectations isn't giving up. It's letting go. Of outcomes. Of things that are beyond our control. Of the belief that life is going to be—or even should be—a trouble-free, smooth ride toward bliss and adulation.

That's not how things work, and it's okay. The sooner we embrace this unavoidable reality, the sooner we can focus on living in it. Consider what Jonathan Rauch, the author of *The Happiness Curve*, told me: "When we accept that we won't be rock stars or astronauts, that is when we start to see the good with our normal lives." Letting go of fame as the metric of success liberates us to savor the daily satisfaction that comes from playing the guitar instead of hoping that music will win us the spotlight, money, and a sauna full of groupies.

Lowering expectations doesn't mean you don't want to win. It means pursuing victory in the forms of unsexy but deeply meaningful and sustainable rewards. It's focusing on financial autonomy instead of vast wealth. It's working toward "healthy" as opposed to "skinny." It's striving for improvement over perfection.

Yes, you should still work hard, but only in pursuit of "right side" goals. Choose to win by prioritizing a lifestyle that leads to contentment and peace of mind. Your nights might not be sexy, but you'll feel more secure in yourself—and you probably don't want to find out what's lurking in celebrity jacuzzis, anyway.

Don't Live Every Day as if it's Your Last

How a health scare put YOLO into context
SUBSTACK, JUNE 2022

A while back, after two good friends suffered fatal heart attacks, I booked an appointment for a calcium scan, an MRI-like procedure that detects blockage of the arteries. Then 46-years-old, I had tons of energy and worked out almost daily. So I was surprised when the test results indicated that I have coronary artery disease. CAD is a serious condition that requires vigilance but can be managed pretty effectively for decades with exercise, a healthy diet, and Lipitor or other cholesterol-inhibiting statins.

Shortly after my diagnosis, I shared the news with a friend. He replied with great conviction, "Bro, you just need to live every day as if it's your last day on earth!"

With due respect to my friend's enthusiasm, warm intentions, and SoCal vibes, this is terrible advice. As much as it fits with the YOLO subculture's approach to making the most out of life, none of us should conduct ourselves as if there is no tomorrow. It's a bad idea on many levels.

Living each day as if it's your last is a self-fulfilling proposition. Just ask the extreme athletes who died performing stunts for Red Bull: they went sky-diving and heli-skiing, then learned the hard way that—contrary to the brand slogan—Red Bull does *not* give you wings. These brazen competitors did some crazy-cool shit, but now they're dead.

Don't get me wrong—I'm all for living life to the fullest, but part of that equation means staying alive as long as possible. The other day, a friend of mine posted to Facebook an inspirational quote from Amelia Earhart. It read: "Use your fear. It can take you to the place where you store your courage."

Here's another, more recent Amelia Earhart quote: "Arrrrrrggghhhhh! I should have listened to my fear!"

Okay, that's a little mean, and I acknowledge that we're still talking about her 83 years after her death, so she was obviously a courageous trailblazer. But think of how much more she would have accomplished if she had stuck around another few decades, or at least into her mid-forties.

To be clear, I don't recommend covering yourself in bubble wrap and taking shelter in a germ-free saferoom. Daily interactions with the world require some risk-taking (I almost got run over the other day by a teenager on a Bird scooter in the Kroger parking lot). However, accepting that we will die and inviting an early death are two very different things, so let me restate my theoretical guideline more clearly:

Do stop and smell the roses.

Do tell your friends you love them.

Do practice gratitude through meditation or prayer.[3]

Don't go base-jumping. In fact, if you ever find yourself strapping a GoPro camera to your chest, stop and ask yourself, "Is this a good idea?" I guarantee you it's not.

There's an old Southern street joke that goes like this:

Q: *What's the last thing you hear a redneck say?*

A: *Hey y'all, watch this!*

We don't know what this good ol' boy is fixin' to do, but it's sure to be foolish. Whether he's about to guzzle a flaming jug of moonshine or launch his F-150 over a crick, *Dukes of Hazzard* style, we can bet that he will end up deceased.

In the same way, when someone breaks out their GoPro, they're screaming, "Hey Instagram, watch this!" Since nobody on Instagram is going to share a video of them doing their taxes early or prudently

---

3   In your own space, not on the public high school football field.

applying sunscreen to their ear lobes, the GoPro accurately foreshadows a premature death.

Living each day as if it's your last isn't just unsafe, it also threatens your legacy. How you live those final 24 hours will be the subheading on your obituary, and you don't want it to read, "Died penniless, surrounded by strippers, and covered in vomit."

Consider Elvis Presley. He recorded 100 gold records, starred in dozens of movies, lived in a mansion, owned limousines, and private jets, and dated Ann Margaret, Mary Tyler Moore, Cybill Shepherd, and numerous other starlets.

Yet how did the King of Rock n' Roll spend his last day? By dying on the toilet.

Every day is precious, the future is unknown, and life will be over way sooner than most of us think. So make it count. But, you know, stay off pills, wear your seat belt, and get some fiber in your diet.

Your Only Goal Is to Arrive

To survive quarantine, you need to change your metrics
MEDIUM, APRIL 2020

When our son was one year old, my pregnant wife and I endured a grueling day of travel from northern Michigan to Los Angeles, where we lived at the time. A canceled flight and a missed connection led to five hours in the Detroit airport with a squirmy child whose undiagnosed ear infection had kept any of us from sleeping the night prior.

The fun was just beginning when the flight finally took off. As changes in cabin pressure inflicted cochlear agony, my son didn't just cry—he let loose desperate, primal screams that could not be extinguished with hugs, Juicy Juice, or M&M's. His anguish was so extreme that fellow passengers zoomed right past anger and straight to incredulous pity. Somewhere over Wyoming, the kind woman next to us held the demon boy and his attention by pointing at clouds out the window. Finally, after a 16-hour travel day, we landed at LAX and sheepishly mumbled our apologies and thanks to those around us.

The next morning, I shared my hellish tale with my colleague Jen, whose older children had taught her parenting strategies I hadn't yet learned. I also apologized for not working on the project I was supposed to review over the weekend.

"Don't worry about it," Jen said. "When you travel with babies, your only goal is to arrive."

I asked her to elaborate. "Well, traveling with kids is a whole different thing than traveling by yourself," she said. "Forget about napping, reading a book, or checking email. Your only job is to keep the baby safe and as comfortable and quiet as possible. If you show up with your children alive, you've succeeded."

I kept this simple yet profound concept in mind during 100% of our subsequent trips with our young children. It didn't make those flights fun per se, but the mantra helped to keep my priorities in line.

During the pandemic, I read an article encouraging people to use the quarantine to achieve something "extraordinary" with their lives. Jen's advice came screaming back to mind. Today's flight, dear friends, is very much delayed: not by hours, but months. Travel conditions are—to put it mildly—suboptimal. Each of us should have in mind only one goal: to arrive on the other side in one piece.

Even with the coronavirus in the review mirror, our reality has changed. We know now that we need to change the metrics by which we judge our success. If *Satisfaction=Experience–Expectations*, and much of the experience is out of our control, now is the time to make sure our expectations are realistic and achievable.

Expect delays in life. Expect crying babies. Expect to sit on the tarmac of human biology for most of the summer, staring out the window at a cloudless sky, thinking, "Why the hell aren't we taking off?" The flight crew will run out of peanuts, headphones, and Sprite Zero. The toilets will overflow, and—as we already know—toilet paper will disappear.

Your job is to maintain sanity, stay healthy, and—where you can—offer kindness to your fellow flyers. (No, this metaphor doesn't mean you have to hold someone else's baby for a few months.) Only a realistic clarity of mission will keep you above the fray. Your neighbors will freak out. In our climate of the 24-hour news cycle, journalists will constantly predict the end of the world. And the same children who used to terrorize you on planes will now force you to watch *High School Musical 2* over and over.

Perhaps most insidious of all, motivational gurus will preach at you to *carpe* that *diem* and use every opportunity to write your novel, reclaim your beach body, or run a marathon in your living room.

Granted, there are a small number of ninjas who could learn calligraphy in a POW camp or write a bestseller in coach class. But for the rest of us, we should always keep our goals reasonable. When you're trying to hang onto a job or file for unemployment while raising kids, arranging care for an elderly parent, and bathing only occasionally, you are already operating at a very high level.

So forgive yourself for the three dinners you had last night, the gray roots, and that goofy home haircut. (It's a great time to be bald!) Forget the motivational nonsense, and—for the love of all things self-preserving—turn off the gosh-darn news. Here, I'll summarize it for you: things are bad. They're going to stay bad for quite a while. We'll text you when it's over. In the meantime, relax. No, I don't advocate numbing yourself until August, but if you need a glass of chardonnay, a half-pint of Chunky Monkey, or a full season of *Tiger King* to get you through, go for it. Just make sure these remain a "treat" and not your baseline (or breakfast).

There are undeniable superheroes out there right now. But for most of us, our role is to stay home and care for ourselves and those around us. We can do our best within the controllable elements of the experience: get eight hours of sleep. Meditate. Stretch. Take a walk (while keeping your distance). Secure your own mask first.

If you've got that covered, look for ways to brighten someone else's day. Write a thank-you note to the mail carrier. Leave the sanitation workers Gatorade and some antibacterial wipes. If you have an extra few bucks, donate to the local food bank. But don't ever beat yourself up about "living your best life," or start a real estate business in your pajamas.

When the plane finally lands, no one around you is going to remember if you finished that book proposal. All they'll care about is whether you maintained your cool and kept your child from puking all over their chinos. Take it from an insecure workaholic who has, for far too long, equated self-worth with productivity: it's not about what you get done right now. This journey is going to be arduous. Anything you accomplish beyond making it through in one piece is gravy.

You know what will be exceptional? Surviving and arriving.

Acknowledgements

One of the things you hear a lot in wellness literature and podcasts these days is the encouragement to avoid comparing oneself to others. Instead, they encourage the audience to "Measure yourself against who you were yesterday" or something along those lines. I find great wisdom in this advice.

Part of what this book represents to me is my growth as a writer over the past decade. In reviewing some of the earlier pieces that didn't make the cut, I was reminded how far I've come in those years. Not that the newer pieces are on par with William Shakespeare or Danielle Steele, but the contrast between the old and new demonstrated notable improvement in technique and sincerity. My improvement has been the result of many factors, including practice, voracious reading, and coaching of two guys in particular.

Shortly after I left Facebook in 2011, my former colleague and friend, Jesse Dwyer encouraged me to write and speak. I didn't know how to go about it, but—with his guidance—I started by starting. I proved to be an undisciplined student and even worse client, but many of the essays herein are the direct result of the work Jesse and I did long ago. I remain grateful for his counsel and friendship.

Adam Robinson of Good Book Developers has been my go-to guy for feedback on writing projects since 2015. I picked him off of a website because he lived near me and his glasses made him look much smarter than me, which he is. Most importantly, Adam is an intellectual gut-check who pushes me to be a better writer and a more accountable opiner. We disagree a lot but with the mutual respect that is largely missing in public dialog. I greatly value his input and opinion.

The writing is how it started but the podcast is how the writing reached a wider audience. So I must declare my thanks to guy who convinced me to start *Crazy Money*. As early as 2014, Mike Carano was telling me I should do a podcast about money. It sounded preposterous and I lacked conviction, but five years later he finally convinced me. Mike became not just an editor but a sounding board and conduit to some of my best guests, including Dr. Drew and Judd Apatow. My only regret is that I didn't take his advice earlier.

I would be remiss to not thank my wife, Stacey who not only loves and supports me and my creative efforts tirelessly, but allows me to write about things others might find too close to home. On our very first date in October, 2004, standing on the roof of Sushi Samba in the West Village, I told her "I'm going to quit my job at Yahoo! and become a stand-up comedian." So, to be clear, she was warned. But she has been down for the journey as much as I could hope any wife would be. Now, about how she loads the dishwasher…

Also, to my children (you know who you are). I love you immensely. When I was a grown, yet single man (prior to October 2004), my mother pushed me not so subtly to get married and have kids. I always thought it was because she believed any other life was sinful and offensive to her religious beliefs. I still believe that, partially. But I know now that she wanted me to have children because she wanted me to know how much I was loved. Turns out, that was a lot.

Lastly, I want to thank you, Dear Reader. I have been wildly fortunate to have a robust group of high-quality friends all through my life. These childhood pals, schoolmates, and former colleagues have supported me with their attention, time, and the money they—i.e., *you*—traded for tickets to comedy shows, Substack subscriptions, and copies of the book in your hand. Without this encouragement, I would have quit long ago. If you've read this far, you are obviously dedicated to an irrational degree. Get a life, weirdo.

About the Author

Paul Ollinger is a comedian, speaker, writer, and podcaster. A former digital media executive, he now spends his time making audiences laugh and think all over the United States and, occasionally, in Canada. He is also the author of *You Should TOTALLY Get an MBA: A Comedian's Guide to Top Business Schools.* Paul lives on the Upper West Side of Manhattan with his wife, two teenagers, and two French bulldogs, Theo and Colonel Tom Parker.

Follow Paul!

www.ingramcontent.com/pod-product-compliance
Lightning Source LLC
Chambersburg PA
CBHW020421010526
44118CB00010B/358